Internet of Things with Raspberry Pi 3

Leverage the power of Raspberry Pi 3 and JavaScript to build exciting IoT projects

Maneesh Rao

BIRMINGHAM - MUMBAI

Internet of Things with Raspberry Pi 3

Commissioning Editor: Gebin George
Acquisition Editor: Prachi Bisht
Content Development Editor: Dattatraya More
Technical Editor: Varsha Shivhare
Copy Editors: Safis Editing, Laxmi Subramanian
Project Coordinator: Shweta H Birwatkar
Proofreader: Safis Editing
Indexer: Tejal Daruwale Soni
Graphics: Jisha Chirayil
Production Coordinator: Aparna Bhagat

First published: April 2018

Production reference: 1260418

Published by Packt Publishing Ltd.
Livery Place
35 Livery Street
Birmingham
B3 2PB, UK.

ISBN 978-1-78862-740-5

www.packtpub.com

`mapt.io`

Mapt is an online digital library that gives you full access to over 5,000 books and videos, as well as industry leading tools to help you plan your personal development and advance your career. For more information, please visit our website.

Why subscribe?

- Spend less time learning and more time coding with practical eBooks and Videos from over 4,000 industry professionals

- Improve your learning with Skill Plans built especially for you

- Get a free eBook or video every month

- Mapt is fully searchable

- Copy and paste, print, and bookmark content

PacktPub.com

Did you know that Packt offers eBook versions of every book published, with PDF and ePub files available? You can upgrade to the eBook version at `www.PacktPub.com` and as a print book customer, you are entitled to a discount on the eBook copy. Get in touch with us at `service@packtpub.com` for more details.

At `www.PacktPub.com`, you can also read a collection of free technical articles, sign up for a range of free newsletters, and receive exclusive discounts and offers on Packt books and eBooks.

Contributors

About the author

Maneesh Rao holds over 7 years of experience in software development, primarily in IoT. He has been a part of Thingworx IoT team. Thingworx is one of the most sought after IoT platforms. Furthermore, he has worked for one of the biggest consumer electronics company in India and developed IoT products for smart homes, smart factories, connected vehicles, and smart consumer appliances. He also assists start-ups in developing IoT products.

With deepest gratitude, I wish to thank Packt for showing trust in me and providing the opportunity to write this book and realize my dream. I'd like to thank the team at Packt who worked closely with me to make this book a success.

Last but not least, I want to thank my loving parents and wife who were always there with me in my endeavors and tasks. I am grateful to them for bearing with me whenever I could not give them my time.

About the reviewer

Thushara Jayawardena, who is driven by curiosity, persistence, and engagement, has explored and acquired many skills and experiences in the computer software and micro electronics domains. He has embedded related ranges from Raspberry Pi to Arduino projects. His software-related projects span across Android, JavaScript frame works(NodeJS and Leaflet), and pass technologies(Heroku and Mongo). His day job is at a leading multinational Swedish ERP vendor in Gothenburg. He's been at IFS world operations for over 16 years, working with various aspects of software development.

Packt is searching for authors like you

If you're interested in becoming an author for Packt, please visit `authors.packtpub.com` and apply today. We have worked with thousands of developers and tech professionals, just like you, to help them share their insight with the global tech community. You can make a general application, apply for a specific hot topic that we are recruiting an author for, or submit your own idea.

Table of Contents

Preface

The **Internet of Things** (**IoT**) is about connecting physical devices over the internet to each other, and making them talk to us. Applications of IoT are smart homes, buildings, connected vehicles, and when scaled up they drives smart cities and manufacturing automation. IoT is currently a growing trend in the technology space, and Raspberry Pi is the perfect board to get started with for building IoT projects. This book covers many of the powerful features of Raspberry Pi and projects, such as weather station, a facial recognition system, a security surveillance system, and learning it the practical way of using Raspberry Pi, sensors, and the cloud.

Who this book is for

This book is for all the technology enthusiasts who want to understand what IoT is all about. The readers require just elementary knowledge of computers, programming, and Raspberry Pi. This book helps the readers to resolve the most challenging part that is interfacing hardware with software and sending data to cloud for visualization and analysis with the hands-on DIY projects. In the end, readers will be able to build state-of-the-art solutions for IoT.

What this book covers

Chapter 1, *Introduction to IoT*, provides an introduction to Internet of Things, a little background, the current scenario, the future of IoT, as well as its impact on our life. Here, you will also learn about the architecture of an IoT ecosystem and its application and benefits in different fields.

Chapter 2, *Know Your Raspberry Pi*, introduces you to Raspberry Pi. Why is this one of the most popular boards for learning and building IoT projects? Here, we will learn about the anatomy of Raspberry Pi, GPIO, and other functionalities. Setting it up includes installing an OS, getting comfortable with Shell commands and its UI, and connecting it to a network/Wi-Fi.

Chapter 3, *Let's Communicate*, makes Raspberry Pi communicate with the cloud/server using protocols such as HTTP and MQTT. We will demonstrate how data transfers between Pi and the cloud.

Chapter 4, *Weather Station*, sets up Raspberry Pi as a weather station, which will measure weather conditions and send the data to a Google spreadsheet for analysis. We will measure the temperature and humidity using sensors connected to GPIO programmatically.

Chapter 5, *Controlling the Pi*, explains how to control actuators, LEDs, and other devices connected to Pi remotely using web apps.

Chapter 6, *Security Surveillance*, explains how to build your own security surveillance system to protect your home/premises from intruders. We will use Raspberry Pi, a camera module, a motion sensor, and cloud to complete this project.

Chapter 7, *Image Recognition*, explains how we can leverage IoT to accomplish complex tasks such as face recognition using Raspberry Pi, camera module, AWS Rekognition, and AWS S3 service.

Chapter 8, *Bot Building*, shows how to build a Wi-Fi-controlled robot car using Raspberry Pi. We will use a motor-driver circuit, a DC motor, and a web application to complete the task.

Chapter 9, *Security in IoT*, talks about why security is the most important aspect of IoT, what the existing threats at the software and hardware level are, and how we can ensure security in our IoT using various practices.

To get the most out of this book

You need to have a basic understanding of how electronics and circuit and systems work in alliance with different hardware components along with some programming experience.

The installation instructions are presented in a quite detailed fashion. However, if you need more insight, you can proceed to the relevant instructional manuals available in the support sections of the hardware's documentation.

Download the example code files

You can download the example code files for this book from your account at www.packtpub.com. If you purchased this book elsewhere, you can visit www.packtpub.com/support and register to have the files emailed directly to you.

You can download the code files by following these steps:

1. Log in or register at `www.packtpub.com`.
2. Select the **SUPPORT** tab.
3. Click on **Code Downloads & Errata**.
4. Enter the name of the book in the **Search** box and follow the onscreen instructions.

Once the file is downloaded, please make sure that you unzip or extract the folder using the latest version of:

- WinRAR/7-Zip for Windows
- Zipeg/iZip/UnRarX for Mac
- 7-Zip/PeaZip for Linux

The code bundle for the book is also hosted on GitHub at `https://github.com/PacktPublishing/Internet-of-Things-with-Raspberry-Pi-3`. In case there's an update to the code, it will be updated on the existing GitHub repository.

We also have other code bundles from our rich catalog of books and videos available at `https://github.com/PacktPublishing/`. Check them out!

Download the color images

We also provide a PDF file that has color images of the screenshots/diagrams used in this book. You can download it here: `https://www.packtpub.com/sites/default/files/downloads/InternetofThingswithRaspberryPi3_ColorImages.pdf`.

Conventions used

There are a number of text conventions used throughout this book.

`CodeInText`: Indicates code words in text, database table names, folder names, filenames, file extensions, pathnames, dummy URLs, user input, and Twitter handles. Here is an example: "The `callback` function is called when an asynchronous function returns its result, whereas events work with an observer pattern."

A block of code is set as follows:

```
const express = require('express');
const app = express();
```

Any command-line input or output is written as follows:

```
npm install
```

Bold: Indicates a new term, an important word, or words that you see onscreen. For example, words in menus or dialog boxes appear in the text like this. Here is an example: "Include the IP address, which your router has provided to your Pi, as the **Host Name (IP address)** and click on **Open**, as shown in *Figure 3.4*."

 Warnings or important notes appear like this.

 Tips and tricks appear like this.

Get in touch

Feedback from our readers is always welcome.

General feedback: Email feedback@packtpub.com and mention the book title in the subject of your message. If you have questions about any aspect of this book, please email us at questions@packtpub.com.

Errata: Although we have taken every care to ensure the accuracy of our content, mistakes do happen. If you have found a mistake in this book, we would be grateful if you would report this to us. Please visit www.packtpub.com/submit-errata, selecting your book, clicking on the Errata Submission Form link, and entering the details.

Piracy: If you come across any illegal copies of our works in any form on the Internet, we would be grateful if you would provide us with the location address or website name. Please contact us at copyright@packtpub.com with a link to the material.

If you are interested in becoming an author: If there is a topic that you have expertise in and you are interested in either writing or contributing to a book, please visit authors.packtpub.com.

Reviews

Please leave a review. Once you have read and used this book, why not leave a review on the site that you purchased it from? Potential readers can then see and use your unbiased opinion to make purchase decisions, we at Packt can understand what you think about our products, and our authors can see your feedback on their book. Thank you!

For more information about Packt, please visit `packtpub.com`.

Introduction to IoT 1

In this chapter, we will understand what the **Internet of Things** (**IoT**) is all about. Also, we will learn about the architecture of an IoT ecosystem, its application and benefits in different fields, its background, the current scenario, and its future.

The topics that we're going to cover are:

- Understanding IoT
- Architecture of an IoT ecosystem
- History and evolution
- IoT applications and future prospects

Understanding IoT

Looking back at the last few years, it can be observed that the Internet of Things (hereafter IoT) has become one of the most revolutionary technologies for research and development. It has opened the floodgates for numerous upcoming business models and assists in reinventing existing businesses.

But what is IoT, anyway? Why has it been called a new technological revolution? Who invented it, and when? What are its applications? Does it really hold the potential to change our lives? We will answer all such questions in this book, not just theoretically but in a DIY way. Yes, that's the best way to learn IoT.

Defining IoT

IoT is not just technology; it is the concept of a whole new world where physical things such as cars, homes, buildings, and other components of cities have the ability to connect to the internet and interact among themselves and with humans as well. In short, it is a smart and connected world.

IoT is a phenomenon that can only be described and not defined as it is an inclusive technology that has unlimited boundaries.

A physical device in an IoT ecosystem is also called a thing or smart thing. A thing can be any device with one or more of the following features:

- Sensors (temperature, humidity, motion detector)
- Communication (wired or wireless)
- Actuators (motor, relay, display)
- Controller or processor (for computations, running software)

A few examples of things are:

- Tags such as NFC, RFID, and QR code, which are computer-readable and used to identify objects
- Devices such as iBeacon, Arduino, and Raspberry Pi, which have built in controllers/processors and communication channels such as Bluetooth, Wi-Fi, Ethernet, and so on
- Machines such as cars, bikes, AC units, and washing machines that can work autonomously
- Infrastructure such as smart-connected factories, smart-connected buildings, and smart cities

Architecture of an IoT ecosystem

Let's understand how an IoT ecosystem works with the help of an example.

Mr. Ghanshyam is the owner of a Cargo company that has a large number of trucks as part of its fleet. They provide transportation services to various other businesses across the country. Lately, he has been incurring losses in his business due to various reasons that he has not been able to identify and rectify.

His son Shyam, who works as an IoT engineer, gets to know about his father's business condition and decides to come down and assist him. He works with him over the next few months and observes a few major issues that are incurring losses. A few of the issues are listed here:

- High fuel consumption
- High maintenance costs

- Delivery delays
- High accident rates

Shyam, being an IoT engineer, knew what needed to be done to make the business profitable and easy to manage. Let's see what steps were carried out.

Shyam converted all the trucks of fleet into smart and connected one by fitting them with various sensors to measure vital stats such as fuel level, tyre pressure, engine condition, temperature, and others. Controllers were used to perform actions as per requirements, such as turning on lights when the sun set, turning on wipers when it rained, alerting drivers, and sending important information to the cloud with the help of Wi-Fi/GPRS/GPS modules over the internet. Cameras and other such devices were used to keep an eye on driver performance to get real-time data from a truck, as shown in the following figure:

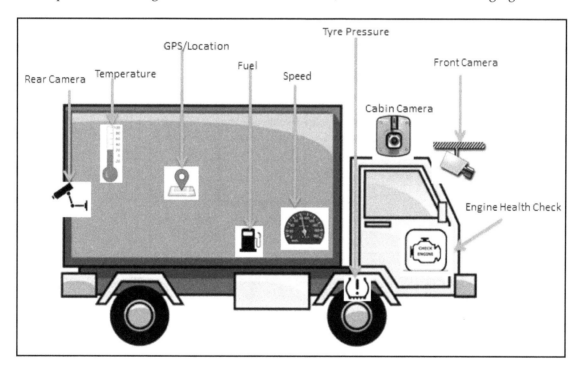

A mobile application was developed to help drivers monitor the truck's condition in real time, navigate via the best route, and receive alert notifications and job/task assignments.

An admin/control panel application was also developed and was used at the command center by managers and operators to monitor all moving trucks, which were sending real-time data over the internet. This facilitated better fleet management in the following ways:

- Monitoring a truck's route to its destination; if the driver is going to a suspicious location, the engine can be turned off remotely.
- Monitoring the driver's conduct with the help of a camera inside his cabin. This avoids incidents of sleeping or talking over the phone while driving and sends an alert immediately.
- Navigating to nearby service stations in the case of a breakdown:

After taking all of the above measures the old fleet had now been converted into smart and connected fleet. The following figure helps us understand the architecture of the IoT solution deployed by Shyam:

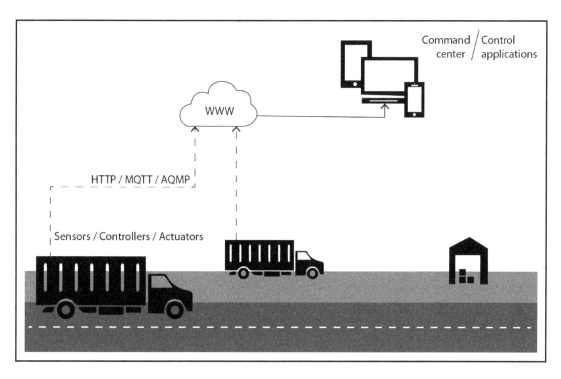

Let's see how smart and connected fleets made Mr. Ghanshyam's business profitable:

- **Fuel efficiency**: Data received regarding braking, shifting gears, and speed helped to establish and improve the driving style of each driver, which in turn improved fuel efficiency. Also, checking on fuel levels periodically helped to curb incidents of fuel theft, which in turn reduced overall fuel cost.

- **Maintenance costs and delivery delays**: The sensors installed in each truck send vital information about engine health, brakes, electrical systems, and oil levels. This helps the operator to maintain the overall health of the vehicle through timely and preventive maintenance, hence reducing frequent breakdowns and delays, leading to substantial cost savings.

- **Improved safety**: Monitoring the driver's conduct using cameras and other sensor data helped detect aggressive, careless, and improper driving, which is always a threat to driver and vehicle safety. This data could be used to alert the driver, hold him accountable, and provide proper training for future improvement.

- **Route optimization**: By tracking a vehicle's current location and traffic condition using GPS, the shortest and best route could be suggested , resulting in the vehicle reaching its destination in the minimum time, reducing fuel cost, and saving time so more deliveries can be made and in turn increasing profits.
- **Environmental impact**: With improved vehicle conditions and taking an optimized route, lesser fuel is used, leading to less emissions of harmful gases.

Let's now look at the generalized architecture of an IoT ecosystem in the following figure. Here, we also explain the components of this architecture, such as what each component is, what role it plays, and how it is integrated with other components in the whole architecture:

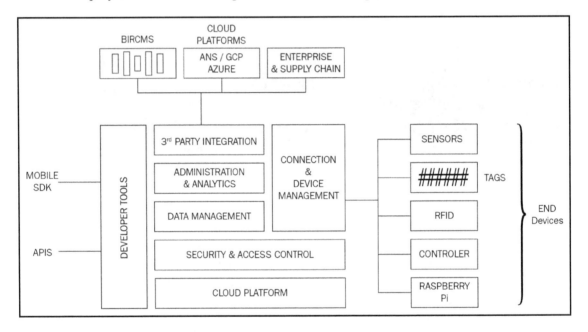

The following is a brief explanation of the general IoT architecture:

- Sensors, tags, and microchips are end devices in the system that observe the environment and provide information about it.
- Connection management takes care of maintaining connectivity between end devices and the user/platform through various protocols such as HTTP, MQTT, and AQMP over the internet, and using Bluetooth and radio frequencies as well.

- Real-time data management helps collect and store data received from end devices in the database, which may be relational or NoSQL based on the type of data.
- Security and access control prevents unauthorized users getting access to the system, which then may be misused. Security is one of the most important building blocks in an IoT ecosystem; neglecting it may cause huge losses for enterprises and individuals.
- Cloud platforms facilitate the scalability, availability, and accessibility of the whole system with minimum downtime, which is very critical for a connected system.
- Administration and analytics components use all the data provided by a device to understand the behavior of the device and end user, which further helps in improving the service, performing preventive maintenance, and providing necessary alerts and notifications.
- Integration with other platforms such as social media, BI, and CMS, and enterprise and supply chain helps to bridge the gap between different segments of business.
- Developer tools help third parties to integrate their existing system seamlessly.

History and evolution

A few decades back, the only way for humans to connect with each other was through personal communications, postal services, and fixed line telephones. Who would have thought about machines talking to each other and to humans as well? But with the introduction of the internet, and advancement in hardware and communication technology, this has become a reality.

The Internet of Things may be a new topic for many of us but its foundation was laid in 1999 by Kevin Ashton of MIT's AutoID lab, when he coined the term Internet of Things while making a presentation at Procter & Gamble.

Today IoT has become the next revolution in the internet world; it harnesses the intelligence of billions of sensors and connected things, which collect big data to make decisions. See the following figure to understand the evolution of IoT over the last few decades:

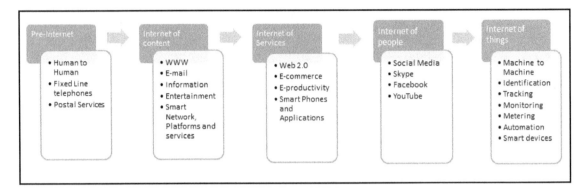

IoT–applications and future prospects

Here are some statistics that show the future prospects of the Internet of Things:

- Gartner, Inc. believes that by 2020 the number of connected devices will reach 25 billion. The Internet of Things has become a powerful force for business transformation, and its disruptive impact will be felt across all industries and all areas of society.
- According to Gartner, Inc., more than 50% of new business processes will contain devices connected to the internet.
- The total economic impact of IoT, including consumer surplus, is estimated to be between $3.9 and $11.1 trillion in 2025.
- According to Nasdaq, there will be close to 80 billion connected devices by 2025.

A detailed view of IoT applications in different industries is represented in the following figure:

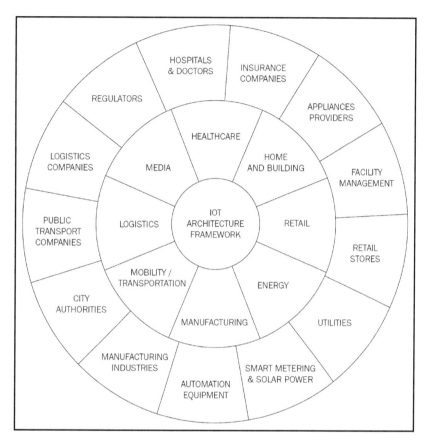

Let's understand in a bit more detail about IoT applications in different industries:

- Household devices such as refrigerators, lighting, washers, and thermostats can be controlled by mobile applications from anywhere. The market for these smart home appliances is expected to grow to $122 billion by 2022.
- Wearable devices such as the Fitbit, which tracks body movement and calorie consumption, have already become mainstream.
- Connected vehicles are already in the market from big players such as Honda, VW, and Tesla, which are leading this sector. Looking at the recent development of self-driving technology, autonomous vehicles no longer remain unimaginable.

- Manufacturing plants and factories will be able to monitor their own health and predict maintenance at the right time, which will increase lifespan with minimal downtime. Manufacturing is expected to be one of the largest contributors to the overall growth of IoT and is projected to reach $913 billion by 2018.
- Power grids and solar plants will be connected to the internet, which will help the distributor supply power more effectively to the end user, keeping track of actual usage and preventing theft, among other benefits.
- Sectors positioned to benefit from IoT growth include:
    - **Connected device manufactures**: Creators of wearables, smart meters, and home appliances
    - **Network providers**: IoT needs fast, secure, and reliable network interconnection for devices and systems
    - **Semi-conductor**: There will be significant demand for microcontrollers, flash devices, and sensors

Summary

In this chapter, we introduced the concept of IoT. Then we went on to delve into the IOT ecosystem and its architecture in depth. We also learnt about its history, evolution, and its bright future.

In `Chapter 2`, *Know Your Raspberry Pi*, we will work with Raspberry Pi, which is one of the most popular and widely used single-board computer systems for hacking IoT.

Know Your Raspberry Pi 2

In this chapter, we will introduce ourselves to Raspberry Pi 3 Model B (hereafter Raspberry Pi) and learn about its anatomy in detail, such as its GPIO, processor, Wi-Fi module, Bluetooth, and other such functionalities and capabilities. After this, we will go through the steps for setting up Raspberry Pi by installing the OS, connecting it to the network/Wi-Fi, and getting comfortable with its GUI and Command Prompt.

The following topics are covered in this chapter:

- Understanding Raspberry Pi 3
- Features of Raspberry Pi 3
- Setting up Raspberry Pi 3

Understanding Raspberry Pi 3

Raspberry Pi is a miniature computer that can pack a serious punch. This single-board computer has no less power than a mid-range desktop. Pi is one of the most widely used boards for IoT projects due to its small size, general purpose input/output pins, Wi-Fi, and Bluetooth:

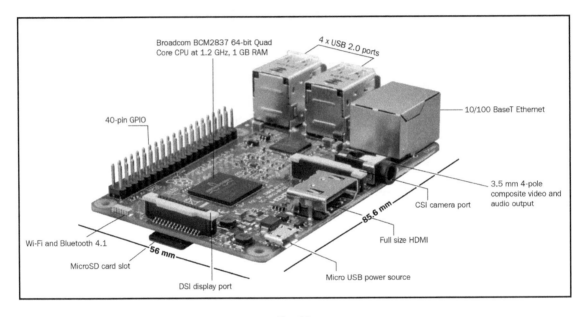

Figure 2.1

Let's list the technical specifications of Raspberry Pi 3 Model B; refer to *Figure 2.1*:

- Broadcom BCM2837 chipset
- 1.2 GHz Quad-Core ARM Cortex-A53
- 802.11 bgn wireless LAN (Wi-Fi) and Bluetooth 4.1 (Bluetooth classic and low energy)
- 1 GB RAM
- 64-bit CPU
- 4 x USB ports
- 40-pin GPIO
- 3.5 mm 4-pole composite video and audio output
- Full size HDMI
- 10/100 BaseT Ethernet

- CSI camera port for connecting the Raspberry Pi camera
- DSI display port for connecting the Raspberry Pi touchscreen display
- MicroSD card slot for loading your operating system and storing data
- Micro USB power source

Important features of Raspberry Pi 3 Model B

The following are the important features:

- **Power**:
    - Raspberry Pi is powered by a +5.0V micro USB supply
    - A 2.5 ampere power supply works well to power Pi and it uses a maximum of 1 amp
    - GPIO pins can draw 50 mA of current in total, distributed across all pins where each pin can draw 16 mA
    - The HDMI port uses a 50 mA current, whereas the camera module draws a 250 mA current
    - A USB-based mouse and keyboard can use 100 mA to 1000 mA current

Backpowering is an issue that occurs when Pi is connected through a USB to a host system (host system can be a laptop or desktop). The host system doesn't have diode protection, which means it backfeeds the power to Pi (gives power to Pi). This power that is backfed to Pi bypasses the voltage protection, causing damage to Pi.

- **USB**:
    - Raspberry Pi 3 Model B is equipped with four USB 2.0 ports. These are connected to the LAN9512 combo hub/Ethernet chip IC3.
    - USB ports enable the attachment of peripherals such as keyboard, mouse, web camera, and other such USB-based devices.
    - It is an **On-the-Go** (**OTG**) USB. The OTG feature allows Pi to work as a host and device interchangeably.
    - Pi has only one root USB bus port. Traffic from all four USB ports is funneled down to this bus, which operates at a max speed of 480 Mbps.

- **GPIO**:

    - **General Purpose Input/Output** (**GPIO**) are a total of 40 pins.
    - Raspberry Pi has a 26-pin header, which can be used as input and output.
    - All 26 pins can receive and transmit data only in digital format.
    - I/O pins range from **GPIO02** to **GPIO27**. Refer to *Figure 2.2*.
    - There are two pins each for **3.3v DC** (pin **01** and pin **17**) and **5v DC** (pin **02** and pin **04**). These pins are used as the power source for the sensor, LEDs, and other such actuators interfaced with Raspberry Pi.
    - There are seven pins assigned as **Ground**, namely pins **06**, **09**, **14**, **20**, **25**, **30**, and **39**, as shown in the following diagram:

Pin#	NAME			NAME	Pin#
01	**3.3v** DC Power			DC Power **5v**	02
03	**GPIO02** (SDA1 , I²C)			DC Power **5v**	04
05	**GPIO03** (SCL1 , I²C)			Ground	06
07	**GPIO04** (GPIO_GCLK)			(TXD0) **GPIO14**	08
09	Ground			(RXD0) **GPIO15**	10
11	**GPIO17** (GPIO_GEN0)			(GPIO_GEN1) **GPIO18**	12
13	**GPIO27** (GPIO_GEN2)			Ground	14
15	**GPIO22** (GPIO_GEN3)			(GPIO_GEN4) **GPIO23**	16
17	**3.3v** DC Power			(GPIO_GEN5) **GPIO24**	18
19	**GPIO10** (SPI_MOSI)			Ground	20
21	**GPIO09** (SPI_MISO)			(GPIO_GEN6) **GPIO25**	22
23	**GPIO11** (SPI_CLK)			(SPI_CE0_N) **GPIO08**	24
25	Ground			(SPI_CE1_N) **GPIO07**	26
27	**ID_SD** (I²C ID EEPROM)			(I²C ID EEPROM) **ID_SC**	28
29	**GPIO05**			Ground	30
31	**GPIO06**			**GPIO12**	32
33	**GPIO13**			Ground	34
35	**GPIO19**			**GPIO16**	36
37	**GPIO26**			**GPIO20**	38
39	Ground			**GPIO21**	40

Figure 2.2

- GPIO pins can be configured to provide alternate functions such as SPI, PWM, I²C, and UART, which we will cover shortly.

- I^2C: Since Raspberry Pi has a limited number of GPIOs, we might need more I/O pins in the case of measuring systems. To overcome this, I/O expander chips are used and interfaced with the I^2C pins/bus of Raspberry Pi. I^2C allows multiple devices to connect to the same bus. Refer to *Figure 2.3*. Two dedicated pins are provided in Pi **GPIO02** and **GPIO03** (refer to *Figure 2.2*). **GPIO02** is an SDA, which is the data line, and **GPIO03** is SCL, which is a signal used to synchronize all data transfers via the I^2C bus:

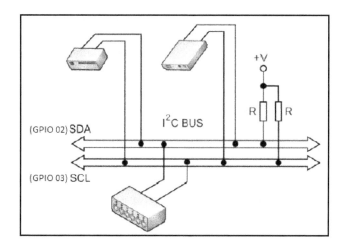

Figure 2.3

UART stands for **Universal Asynchronous Receiver/Transmitter**. It is an asynchronous serial communication protocol, which receives the data in bytes and transmits the individual bits in a sequential manner. Due to its asynchronous nature, it allows users to send data without clock signals; instead, start and end bits are used to synchronize the data transfer. Two pins are defined in Pi for UART communication, **GPIO14** (**TXD**) for transmitting data and **GPIO15** (**RXD**) for receiving data. UART is used to interface devices such as Arduino and ESP8266, and also to get access to kernel boot messages from the serial console.

SPI stands for **Serial Peripheral Interface**. It is a communication protocol used to transfer data between Raspberry Pi and peripheral devices connected to it, such as sensors and actuators. Let's understand with an example how SPI communicates with analog to digital converters.

SPI uses four dedicated pins for communication. These are marked as **Serial Clock (CLK, GPIO011)**, **Master Input Slave Output (MISO, GPIO09)**, **Master Output Slave Input (MOSI, GPIO10)**, and **Chip Select (CS, GPIO08 ,GPIO07)**.

The clock pin reads the input signal at regular frequency, which is the rate at which data transfer takes place between Pi and ADC.

MISO is the data pin used by the master (Raspberry Pi) to receive data from the slave (ADC).

MOSI is used by the master to send data to the slave.

When multiple peripherals are connected to the same SPI bus chip, selective pins are used to make one peripheral active at a time and to transfer data and ignore the rest of the devices.

PWM stands for **Pulse Width Modulation**. It is a technique for controlling outgoing power to connected peripherals. For example, we can control the speed of the DC motor using PWM. There are two PWM channels available in Raspberry Pi, GPIO12 and GPIO19.

The following are the different ports for Raspberry Pi 3 Model B:

- **Audio/video port**: It has a 3.5 mm 4-pole composite audio and video port. This single port carries both audio and video signals. It is a **Tip Ring Ring Sleeve** (**TRRS**) type connector.
- **HDMI port**: It has a full-size HDMI port. Any monitor/TV can be connected to Pi directly.
- The 10/100 BaseT Ethernet port in Pi is used to connect to the internet through a cable. It has the capability of transmitting data at 10 and 100 Mbps.
- **CSI Camera port**: It also has a **Mobile Industry Processor Interface** (**MIPI**) camera serial interface. It facilitates connection to small camera modules directly on board.
- **DSI Display Port**: It is a high-speed serial interface. It has a very low voltage swing of up to 200mV only, which helps to curb electromagnet noise and consume less power.
- **Wi-Fi and Bluetooth**: It also includes Broadcom BCM43438 Wi-Fi and a Bluetooth combo chip. Both are implemented on the same chip as completely independent capabilities. The Wi-Fi adaptor is 802.11b/g standard and has a data transfer speed of up to 72.2 Mbps. The same chip has Bluetooth 4.1 and Bluetooth Low Energy.
- **Memory card slot**: A push-pull micro SD card slot for a memory card is included. Since Pi doesn't have any onboard storage/flash, the OS is installed on a micro SD card and is used for other storage purposes.

All of the previous descriptions should have given you a fair bit of knowledge about your Raspberry Pi hardware, technical specifications, functionalities, and other capabilities.

Setting up Raspberry Pi

We will use the following items to complete the setup:

- A Raspberry Pi 3 Model B.
- A monitor for display, preferably with HDMI connectivity. If your monitor supports only VGA, you can use a VGA to HDMI converter.
- A keyboard and mouse that can be connected to Pi through USB.
- A MicroSD card and card reader. Since Pi doesn't have onboard storage, we will install the OS on the SD card itself, so at least 8 GB is preferable.
- **A power supply**: Raspberry Pi is powered by micro USB. Use a good adapter with a 2.5 A rating.

If you do not have a keyboard, mouse, and monitor, you can still set up using a headless approach and move to the next topic directly. For now, let's start by setting up Pi using a keyboard, mouse, and monitor.

Install the OS on your SD card. We will install the Raspbian version of the OS here:

1. The best way to install an OS is through **New Out of the Box Software (NOOBS)**.
2. Put your SD card in your computer or SD card reader.
3. Download NOOBS from Raspberry Pi's official website. The download link is `https://www.raspberrypi.org/downloads/noobs`.
4. Select the **Offline and network install** option shown in *Figure 2.4*:

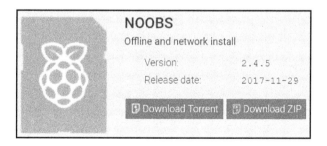

Figure 2.4

5. Now format the SD as FAT. Based on your computer's OS, you can follow the link to format your SD card:

   `https://www.raspberrypi.org/documentation/installation/noobs.md`

6. Extract the ZIP file and transfer all the content onto the SD card. Remove the SD card from your computer and insert it into Raspberry Pi's SD card slot.

7. Power on the Raspberry Pi after connecting a monitor, keyboard, and mouse to it. You will see the NOOBS screen (refer to *Figure 2.5*) with the option of the OS you want to install. Nowadays, only Raspbian is available in a NOOBS installation:

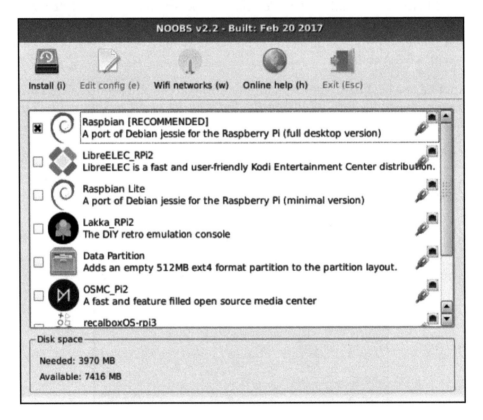

Figure 2.5

8. At the bottom, please select your preferred language and keyboard style.

9. Click on the checkbox next to **Raspbian [RECOMMENDED]**, then click on **Install**. It will take 10–20 mins to complete the installation process.

10. After the completion of the installation process, the GUI will open up, just like in *Figure 2.6*:

Figure 2.6

11. Configure the username, password, and hostname from Raspberry Pi's **Configuration** tab by clicking on **Preferences** under **Menu**, as shown in *Figure 2.7*:

Figure 2.7

12. In the **Raspberry Pi Configuration** window, click on the **System** tab and provide a **Hostname**, **Password**, and **Username** as shown in *Figure 2.8*:

Figure 2.8

13. On the **Interfaces** tab, we can enable **I2C**, **SPI**, serial communication, and also **SSH** and **VNC** to log in to Pi remotely, as shown in the following screenshot:

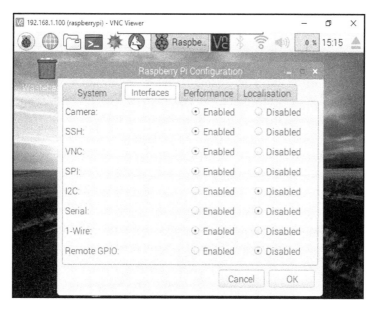

Figure 2.9

Connecting to the internet

Now, we will connect our Raspberry Pi to the Wi-Fi network:

1. In the top-right corner of the GUI, there is a network symbol; click on that.
2. It will show you all the available Wi-Fi networks. You can select the one you want to connect to by providing the password.

3. Now you are good to connect your Pi to the outside world through the internet:

Figure 2.10

4. To verify the internet connectivity, you can try to open any web page or run the `ifconfig` command from the Terminal/Command Prompt, as shown in the following screenshot:

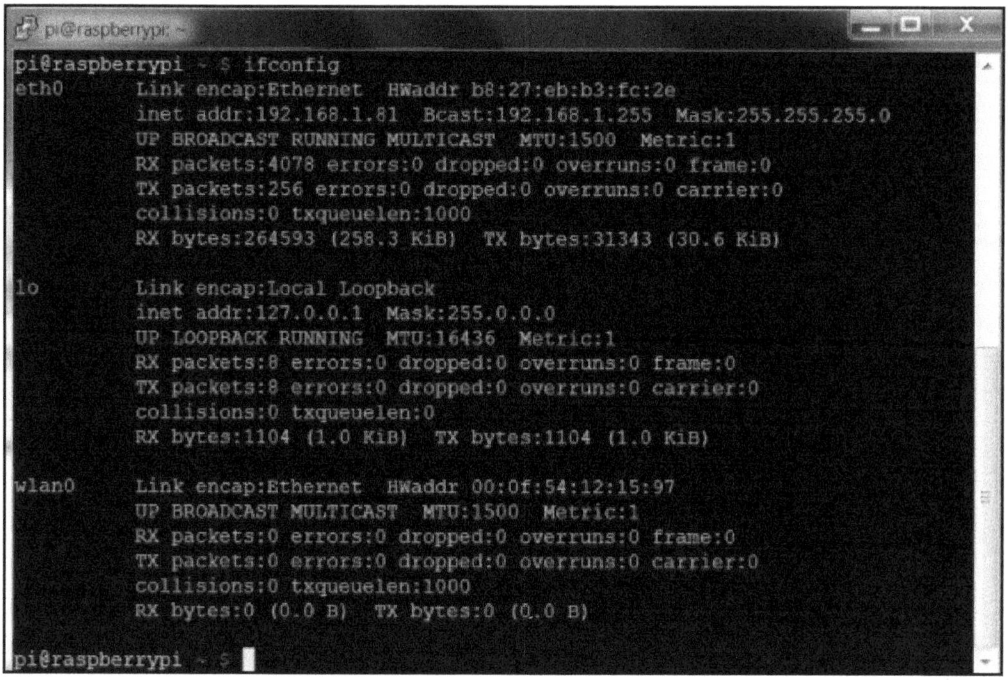

Figure 2.11

Setting up headless Raspberry Pi

Refer to the following steps:

1. Download the Raspbian Lite OS from Raspberry Pi's website at `https://www.raspberrypi.org/downloads/raspbian/`.

2. Once we have the OS image downloaded, we write it to the SD card using a laptop/desktop. Follow the instructions given at: `https://www.raspberrypi.org/documentation/installation/installing-images/README.md` for the OS of your laptop/desktop.

3. To enable SSH on Raspberry Pi, create an empty file with the name `ssh` without any extension. Place this file in the root partition of the SD card.

4. Take out the SD card and insert it into Raspberry Pi. Connect your Ethernet cable from the router to Pi to provide an internet connection and power it up.

5. To connect to Pi using SSH, we need tools such as PuTTY and Advanced IP Scanner. Download and install both the tools from the following links:

   - **PuTTY**: http://www.putty.org/
   - **IP Scanner**: https://www.advanced-ip-scanner.com/

6. Open up the **Advanced IP scanner** and click on the **Scan** button in the top-left corner of the window. A list of all the devices connected to the network appears with their IP addresses. Note down the IP address of Raspberry Pi:

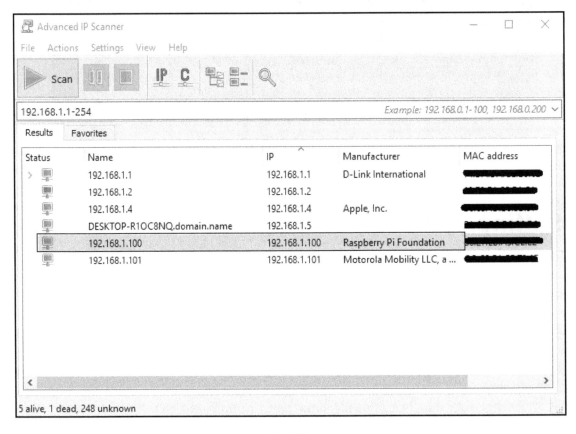

Figure 2.12

7. Use the IP address of Pi from the previous step to connect using PuTTY; open PuTTY by executing `putty.exe`. Enter the IP address as the hostname and click on **Open**:

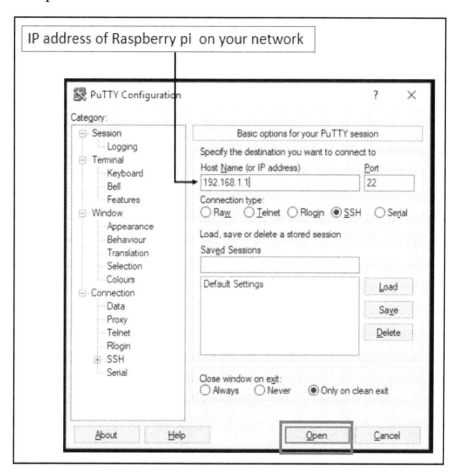

Figure 2.13

8. On first attempt to connect, a warning will appear; just click on **Yes**, since we are connecting to our own Pi:

Figure 2.14

9. On successful connection, a Terminal window will pop up as shown in the following screenshot. If logging in for the first time, enter pi as the username and raspberry as the password:

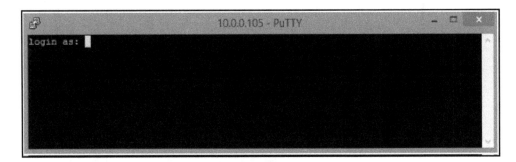

Figure 2.15

10. Upon successful login, the following screen will appear:

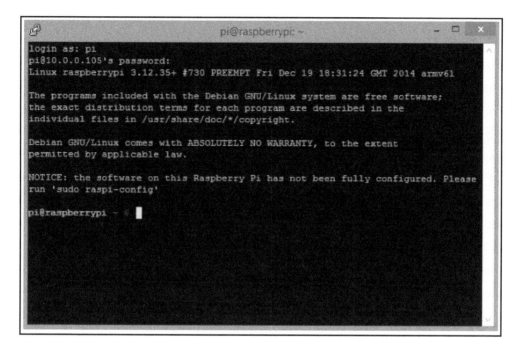

Figure 2.16

Now, you are good to go further and explore.

Summary

In this chapter, we learned about the all-important hardware components of Raspberry Pi 3 Model B in detail. Also, we went through the different functionalities and capabilities of this pocket-sized personal computer.

We walked through the setup of Pi by installing the OS and connecting it to the network, and got familiar with the GUI as well.

In Chapter 3, *Let's Communicate*, we will learn about various communication protocols, which is one of the most important parts of an IoT ecosystem.

3
Let's Communicate

In this chapter, we will learn about important communication protocols such as HTTP and MQTT, which are widely used in IoT architecture. We will also introduce you to the JavaScript programming language and understand why it is becoming the choice for developing IoT applications. We will also demonstrate the implementation of protocols using JavaScript and establish communication between Raspberry Pi and the cloud/server programmatically.

The following topics will be covered in this chapter:

- The internet
- Rise of JavaScript and Node.js
- HTTP
- MQTT
- MQTT brokers

The internet

Before we dive into understanding communication protocols, let's understand how the internet works since it is the backbone in the concept of IoT.

The internet is a global network of computers/systems connected to each other. Each system/computer has a unique **Internet Protocol** (**IP**) address as its identifier over the internet. But how exactly does one system interact with another? Through a protocol stack. It is also referred to as the **Transmission Control Protocol** (**TCP**) or IP protocol stack.

This table will help you understand TCP/IP:

Layer	Description
Application protocol	Specific to application such as FTP, email, HTTP, MQTT, Socket, and the others.
Transmission control protocol	It is a standard that defines how to establish and maintain a connection between applications so that data transmission can take place.
Internet protocol	It directs the message/packet to a specific system using an IP address.
Hardware	It converts binary data packets into network signals.

Let's demonstrate with the help of a diagram how the data flows between two systems over the internet. Say we want to transfer the data from **computer 1** to **computer 2** over the internet. Consider *Figure 3.1*:

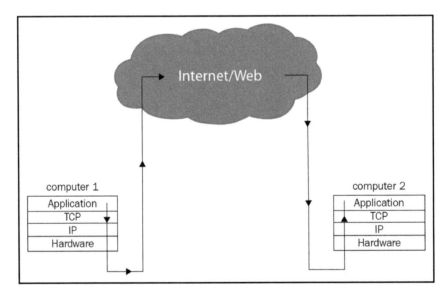

Figure 3.1

1. The data/message starts from the **Application** layer of the computer in the form of a data packet.

2. Then the packet moves down to the **TCP** layer, where it is assigned a port. The port is important because a destination computer might have multiple applications running on different ports, so the packet transmitted from **computer 1** must know the port number of the application running on **computer 2** that is supposed to receive the packet.

3. The packet arrives at the **TCP** layer, where it receives the **IP** address of the destination computer (**computer 2**).

4. Now the data packet has an **IP** address and port number, it is ready to be sent to the destination. The **Hardware** layer is responsible for converting the data in text format to electrical signals, which are then transmitted to the destination over the internet through different modes such as Wi-Fi, Ethernet, and GPRS.

5. Since the destination computer is connected to the internet, it receives the signals being converted to text format in the **Hardware** layer and then moves up to the IP layer, where the IP address is stripped; and then to TCP, where the port is removed from the data packet; and finally to the application layer, where the packet is received and interpreted.

The rise of JavaScript and Node.js

JavaScript, being a dynamic language, is processed by all browsers asynchronously and provides a seamless UI/UX experience for users. JavaScript has become the de facto language for building client-side applications as it supports almost all web standards and protocols.

Since the introduction of runtime Node.js in 2009 by Ryan Dahl, JavaScript has become one of the most favored choices for building large-scale backend applications. Applications that are data intensive, real time, and have high input/output operations are ideal use cases for JavaScript with the Node.js environment. Let's understand Node.js in more depth.

Node.js

Node.js is a JavaScript runtime built on Google's V8 JavaScript engine. It is open source and built to run on all platforms. It provides an event-driven, non-blocking input/output model which makes it very light, fast, and efficient. Applications built using Node.js are scalable and have very high throughput.

Advantages of using Node.js for IoT

The advantages of using Node.js for IoT are as follows:

- **Fast**: Code written in JavaScript executes extremely fast, which enables you to build scalable and network-intensive applications. Google's V8 engine compiles the JavaScript directly into assembly code, ready for execution by the processor.

- **Asynchronous and event-driven**: All requests to the server application written in Node.js are handled in asynchronous/non-blocking fashion. The server never waits for request/API calls to return and it moves to serve the next request. Event or callback functions are used to get responses for previously called requests/APIs once their execution is complete. This helps in maintaining a high level of concurrency and a high input/output rate. Events and callbacks are similar but they operate in a different manner. The `callback` function is called when an asynchronous function returns its result, whereas events work with an observer pattern. Whenever an event is fired, its `listener` function starts execution.

- **Single threaded**: Node.js follows a single-threaded mechanism with event looping. As soon as the Node server is started, it initializes variables and functions and then waits for events to take place. Consider *Figure 3.2* to understand event-driven programming. There is a main loop in a node server application that listens for events/requests and then triggers the `callback/listener` function:

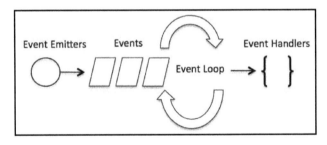

Figure 3.2

- **No buffering**: While processing and uploading the images, audio, and video files, a Node.js application never buffers the files; it just transmits data in chunks, which reduces lot of overhead in processing and reduces the time taken.

- **Open source**: Node.js is open source and has a large community base that supports it. It has an excellent package manager as well, name `npm`.

Let's now understand the different protocols used in the application layer.

HTTP

The **Hyper Text Transfer Protocol** (**HTTP**) is one of most widely used application protocols for communicating over the internet. HTTP is a request-response, client-server protocol, where a client sends a request to a server for information and the server respond with the results.

HTTP is a stateless protocol. When a client sends a request to the server, it maintains a connection with the server only until the server responds or a connection times out. For each request, a new connection must be established. With the help of the diagram in *Figure 3.3*, let's understand response-request architecture:

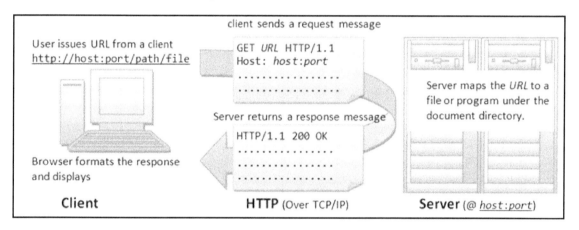

Figure 3.3

The client sends a request to the server. A request consists of the HTTP version, HTTP method, URL, and arguments or the message body:

- The **Uniform Resource Locator** (**URL**) consists of four parts:
    - **Protocol**: It is the application-level protocol used by the client for sending the request to the server
    - **Hostname**: It is the IP address of the server
    - **Port**: The TCP port on which the specific application is running on the server
    - **Path**: It is the path to the specific resource under the target application

- A message body/argument can be text or JSON data that contains information about the client, such as sensor data or customer information, which is being sent to the server as part of the request.
- The URL and message combine to form an HTTP request which is sent to the server over TCP/IP.

The two most commonly used HTTP methods for sending requests are:

- GET: It is used only to retrieve data/information from server without modifying it
- POST: It is used to send data to server such as the status of the device, customer information, and other such details

The server receives and parses the request. Based on the port and path, it maps it to the correct resource and after performing the necessary computation, it prepares the response and sends it back to the client.

The response consists of the status code and the message body. As shown in *Figure 3.3*, the response will have the status code 200 Ok and the message body containing the result expected by the client.

Common response code types are:

- 2xx: Success
- 4xx: Client error
- 5xx: Server error

Implementing HTTP

The following two task will demonstrate how to establish communication between Raspberry Pi and the server using HTTP:

1. Create a HTTP server on a desktop/laptop (called a server hereafter)
2. Create a HTTP client on Raspberry Pi using Node.js

HTTP server

We will make use of the Express framework, which is one of the most popular web frameworks used with Node.js. Please take this as an exercise to learn the Express.js web framework. Follow these steps and at the end, you will have the HTTP server up and running:

1. Since our server is a 64-bit Windows machine, we will download the latest Node.js installer from the official website: `https://nodejs.org/en/download/`. You can install Node.js as per the server configuration and OS.

2. After downloading the installer, run it and complete the installation. The installer will also download **Node Package Manager** (**NPM**) which is used to download and manage additional packages for Node.js development.

3. To check the successful installation of the node and `npm`, execute the following command in the Command Prompt:

   ```
   node -v
   ```

4. This will give you version of Node.js installed:

   ```
   npm -v
   ```

5. This will print the version of `npm` installed.

6. Now, create a folder with the name `HttpServer`, where we will place our code files.

7. Open **Command Prompt** as an administrator and move to the `HttpServer` folder:

8. To make sure we have our environment set up at the `local` folder level, run the following command:

   ```
   npm init
   ```

9. It will help us create `package.json`. This file contains all the metadata relevant to the Node project. A few questions will be asked in order to set up `package.json`, as shown in the following screenshot:

```
D:\HttpServer>npm init
This utility will walk you through creating a package.json file.
It only covers the most common items, and tries to guess sensible defaults.

See `npm help json` for definitive documentation on these fields
and exactly what they do.

Use `npm install <pkg> --save` afterwards to install a package and
save it as a dependency in the package.json file.

Press ^C at any time to quit.
name: (HttpServer) package.json
version: (1.0.0)
description: http server
entry point: (index.js) server.js
test command:
git repository:
keywords:
author: Maneesh
license: (ISC)
About to write to D:\HttpServer\package.json:

{
  "name": "package.json",
  "version": "1.0.0",
  "description": "http server",
  "main": "server.js",
  "scripts": {
    "test": "echo \"Error: no test specified\" && exit 1"
  },
  "author": "Maneesh",
  "license": "ISC"
}


Is this ok? (yes) yes

D:\HttpServer>
```

10. To install node modules, run the following command:

    npm install

    This will install node modules at the `local` folder level.

11. Now we are ready to write our HTTP server code. Create a file, `server.js`, in the `HttpServer` folder and add these lines of code:

```
const express = require('express');
const app = express();
```

We include/import the `express` and body-parser modules in the `server.js` file. Express is a web framework used to create webserver and API endpoints.

Merely including modules in code doesn't serve the purpose; we must explicitly install these modules using the `npm` command as shown here:

`npm install express –save`

```
const server = app.listen(8080, function(){
var host = server.address().address;
var port = server.address().port;
console.log ("Example app listening at http://%s:%s", host,
port);
})
```

12. Here, we provide a port number on which our HTTP server will listen, and also this to on the console.

13. Now, we will create an API route/path, which will act as the endpoint for the client to reach the server. We will use HTTP GET and POST:

```
app.get('/get/information',function(req,res){
console.log("get request received from client") ;
res.send("success") ;
}
```

14. In the GET method, the path or endpoint is `/get/information`. Upon receiving the request from the client on this path, we will print a message on the console and send a response message, `success`, to the client, as a confirmation of the receipt of the request.

15. Let's run the code. Open the Command Prompt, move to the folder (`HttpServer` in our case) where we have the code file, and execute following command:

`node server.js`

16. This is what the actual output upon successful running of your code will look like in Command Prompt:

HTTP client

Since Raspberry Pi acts as our client, we will write our client code in Raspberry Pi itself. Let's install Node.js in our Raspberry Pi. At the end, we will have Node.js up and running. Here, we will SSH into Pi using PuTTY:

1. Open the PuTTY terminal on laptop/desktop.
2. Include the IP address, which your router has provided to your Pi, as the **Host Name (IP address)** and click on **Open**, as shown in *Figure 3.4*:

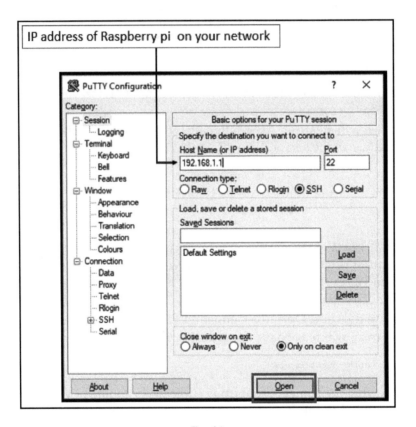

Figure 3.4

3. If you are connecting for the first time, a security warning will appear. Just click **Yes** as shown in *Figure 3.5*, as you are connecting to your own Pi and not a public computer that may harm your system:

Figure 3.5

4. Once you have connected to Pi successfully, you will see the login screen shown in *Figure 3.6*. Log in using the username `pi` and password `raspberry` (if you provided a different username/password while setting up, then use those):

Figure 3.6

5. Since we have successfully logged in through SSH, let's install Node.js now. Create a folder, `nodeDownload`, using the following command:

       mkdir nodeDownload

6. Now move into the newly created folder, using the `cd` command:

       cd nodeDownload/

7. Run the command in the same order:

```
curl -sL http://deb.nodesource.com/setup_8.x | sudo -E bash
sudo apt-get -y install nodejs
```

8. To check that Node.js has successfully installed, use the version command. It will give you the version of node installed:

```
node -v
```

9. Open the terminal window and create a folder under the /home/pi directory with the name piclient, or you can give it any name of your choice. Use this command to create the folder:

```
mkdir piclient
```

10. Before we get into writing our client code, we will repeat step 6 of the previous topic, *HTTP server*, to make sure we have the node module installed and the package.json file at the local folder level.

11. In the terminal window, execute the following command, which will create a file with the name client.js and open it for editing. Here we use the nano editor for creating and editing our file:

```
sudo nano client.js
```

12. Let's start with our client code now:

```
const Client = require('node-rest-client').Client;
var client = new Client();
setInterval(function () {
var sendReq= client.get("http://IP_ADDRESS_OF_HTTP_SERVER :
8080/get/information", function (data) {
console.log("response from server"+data);
});
sendReq.on('error', function (err) {
console.log('request error', err);
});
},5000);
```

13. In the client code, we import the node-rest-client module, which will provide the functionality to send HTTP requests to our HTTP server using methods such as GET and POST.

14. Then, we create a new object for the client to send the request.

15. Use the `setInterval` function of Node.js, which is used to send the request every five seconds.

16. Using a `callback` function, we send the request to the server by providing the complete URL, which includes the public IP address of the server and the path/endpoint. This `callback` function returns the response from the server as the `data` variable, which we print on the console.

17. In case of an error, such as the server not responding and other such issues, we have done error handling on the response from the server.

18. Now, before we run our code, we execute this command in the terminal window to make sure we have the `node-rest-client` module installed locally:

```
npm install node-rest-client –save
```

19. Once done, let's run the client code in the terminal by executing the following command:

```
node client.js
```

20. On successful execution, you will see the output shown in *Figure 3.7*. The client is sending a request to the server every five seconds and getting a successful response:

```
response from server: success :: Wed Oct 25 2017 01:49:43 GMT+0530 (India Standard Time)
response from server: success :: Wed Oct 25 2017 01:49:48 GMT+0530 (India Standard Time)
response from server: success :: Wed Oct 25 2017 01:49:53 GMT+0530 (India Standard Time)
```

Figure 3.7

In this topic, we went through an introduction to the HTTP protocol, did some hands-on implementation, connected Raspberry Pi as a client to the server, and exchanged data between them.

MQTT

MQTT stands for **Message Queue Telemetry Transport**. It is an extremely lightweight messaging protocol based on the publish/subscribe model and favored for use with constrained devices, low bandwidth, or where the network is unreliable.

MQTT was developed by Dr. Andy Stanford Clark of IBM and Arlen Nipper of Arcom (now Eurotech) in 1999. It was designed with the purpose of minimizing the device's resource requirements and network bandwidth consumption, very high scalability, smaller code footprint, and also ensuring the delivery of messages/signals. These attributes of the MQTT protocol make it the right candidate for Internet of Things use cases where we have massive numbers of constrained devices with limited memory, network bandwidth, and less processing power.

MQTT architecture

MQTT works on a publish/subscribe architecture. Publishing is like broadcasting data on a particular channel and subscribing is like listening or receiving the data from a particular channel or source. It is an event-driven communication protocol where messages are pushed to clients; they do not need to pull them from the server as in the HTTP protocol. Here, the central communication server is an MQTT Broker, as seen in *Figure 3.8*:

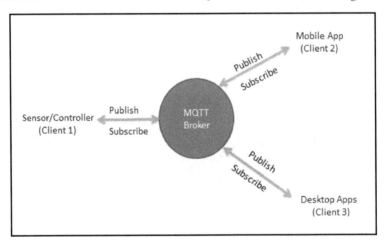

Figure 3.8

The central broker is responsible for dispatching all the messages between senders and receivers. The client/sender after establishing connection with broker publishes a message on a particular topic to a broker (where the topic in MQTT is the routing information for a broker). When a client/receiver subscribes to a topic for receiving messages, the broker diverts all messages with matching topics to the client/receiver. We saw here that there is no direct connection between clients; they communicate on topics without knowing about each other. This architecture helps to build highly scalable IoT solutions.

Let's now look at some important components of the MQTT protocol.

MQTT message types

Three types of message are mostly used:

- CONNECT: Used for clients to send connection requests to the broker
- PUBLISH: Used by the client/sender to publish messages to the broker
- SUBSCRIBE: Used by the client/receiver to receive messages from the broker

MQTT topics

As discussed earlier, a topic is routing information, which is used by the client for publishing and subscribing to messages. Topics are represented by strings and can have one or more levels. Each topic level is separated by a forward slash (/). A topic is created as soon as a client sends data on it, so it is not necessary to create the topic explicitly. Let's understand it with an example. Consider *Figure 3.9*. We have two **Air Conditioners** (**ACs**) at home; one is in the dining room and the other is in the bedroom:

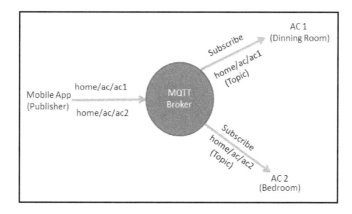

Figure 3.9

Both the ACs are connected to the broker and we have a mobile application that communicates to the AC using the MQTT protocol. The mobile app publishes the message, which can be a control command like temperature change for AC on topics **home/ac/ac1** or **home/ac/ac2**. This topic has three levels: the first one is home, to identify a specific home in a locality or city; the second one is for identifying the type of appliance in the home, which is AC in our case; and the third one is for identifying the particular AC in the house, in our case ac1 for the dining room and ac2 for the bedroom. The broker will send the message to the correct recipient based on topic level.

QoS levels

QoS stands for **Quality of Service**. It is basically a standard for reliability and the successful delivery of each message in MQTT. It makes sure that our messages reach the destination even when a connection is unreliable, and overcomes the issue of data loss. There are three types of QoS as follows:

- **QoS=0**: It just promises to send the message only, once but doesn't ensure its delivery and any retry in case of failure.
- **QoS=1**: It promises that the message will be received by the recipient at least once. Until the sender receives acknowledgement from the recipient, it will keep on sending the message, which can result in duplicate messages.
- **QoS=2**: It promises that message will be received by a recipient only once. It will make sure that there is no data loss or duplication.

Last will and testament

The **Last Will and Testament** (**LWT**) message is used if a client disconnects from a broker unexpectedly. An LWT message is set up and defined at the client side while connecting to the broker for the first time and gets stored at the broker. Whenever a client gets disconnected from the broker abruptly due to network issues or power loss, where the client doesn't get the chance to call the disconnect method to end the connection gracefully, the broker then sends the saved LWT message for that client to all its subscribers, informing them of the sudden unavailability of the client.

Retained messages

When a publisher sends a message on a topic to a broker and no subscriber is listening on that topic, then that particular message will be discarded. Cases where the publisher publishes messages upon state changes such as temperature sensor sends value only when temperature changes then any new subscriber which subscribes to get temperature of this sensor will not get the current value until next change takes place. This can be prevented by sending setting retained flags as `true`, when the publisher connects for the first time to the broker.

Persistent sessions

When a client connects to the broker, it subscribes to certain topics on which it wants to receive messages from the broker. If the client disconnects from the broker, then on reconnect it has to subscribe to all the topics again, which can be a burden for resource-constrained clients. This can be overcome by using a persistent session, which saves all the relevant client-related information on the broker and in the case of reconnection it helps to retain all subscriptions of the client. A client session is stored with respect to `clientId`. The following information is stored in a session:

- All subscriptions
- All messages with QoS 1 and 2 that are not yet acknowledged by the client
- All QoS 1 and 2 messages that the client missed while offline

Keep alive message

In MQTT architecture, clients and brokers connect to each other and send messages to and fro. There is a chance that one of the clients will get disconnected due to an unforeseen issue, such as an unreliable network or a power outage. Such a state is called a half-open connection, where the broker is not aware of the client's unavailability and is trying to send a message and waiting for acknowledgment.

To overcome this issue, MQTT provides the `keep alive` functionality, which assures us that the connection between client and the broker is still alive. The MQTT connect message has the provision of the `keep alive` flag and its value (in seconds) can be set when connecting for the first time to the broker. The `keep alive` time is the maximum timeout between message exchanges. If the broker does not receive a message from the client for a time period of more than 150% of the `keep alive` time, it is considered a half-open connection and the broker will disconnect itself from the client and become free, which saves lots of resources.

So if a client needs to maintain a connection with the broker even if there are no messages to transfer, it must send a `PINGREQ` message within a `keep alive` interval, and the broker responds back with a `PINGRESP` message.

MQTT brokers

There are many open source and paid MQTT brokers available for use, such as:

- Mosquitto
- HiveMQ
- Apache ActiveMQ
- RabbitMQ
- Erlang MQTT (EMQ)

We will use EMQ, which is an open source and massively scalable MQTT broker for connecting our Raspberry Pi to the cloud and communicating with it.

MQTT implementation

Now we will implement the MQTT broker and client.

MQTT broker

Here we will install the EMQ broker on our Windows server, which is our laptop in this case, and create an MQTT client application, which will run on Raspberry Pi:

1. Download a stable release package of the EMQ broker for Windows (or the OS of your server) using this link: http://emqtt.io/downloads.
2. Unzip the downloaded package and place it in any folder of your choice.
3. Open the Command Prompt and move to the `bin` folder of the package using the `cd` command as shown:

```
D:\>cd Maneesh\MQTT\emqttd-windows7-v2.2.0\emqttd\bin
```

4. Start the broker in console mode using the `emqttd` command:

```
D:\Maneesh\MQTT\emqttd-windows7-v2.2.0\emqttd\bin>emqttd console
```

5. On a successful start, the `Erlang` console window will pop up as shown in *Figure 3.10*. If it doesn't, terminate the execution and try again:

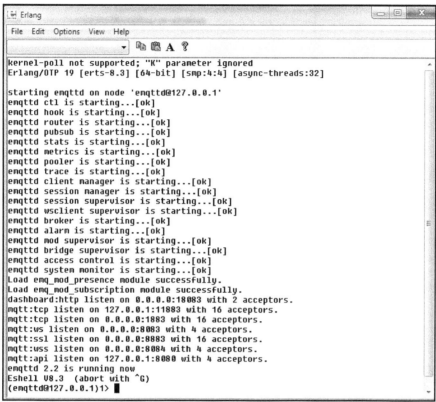

Figure 3.10

6. Now, close the Erlang window and start the MQTT service using the `emqttd start` command. On a successful start of the service, the Command Prompt will come out of the `/bin` folder:

```
D:\Maneesh\MQTT\emqttd-windows7-v2.2.0\emqttd\bin>emqttd start
D:\Maneesh\MQTT\emqttd-windows7-v2.2.0\emqttd>
```

7. Once the MQTT broker is started, we can log in to a web dashboard that comes with broker. We can access the dashboard using these details:

Default Address	http://localhost:18083
Default User	admin
Default Password	public

8. Using **Dashboard**, we can keep track of broker status, clients, topics, sessions, subscriptions, and monitor the statistics and metrics of the broker as shown in *Figure 3.11*:

Figure 3.11

MQTT client

We will create two client applications, one for Raspberry Pi, which will act as the sender (publisher), and one at the server, which will act as the receiver (subscriber). This will help us to implement and better understand the architecture of MQTT. Our implementation will look like the diagram shown in *Figure 3.12*:

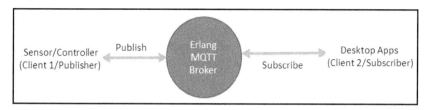

Figure 3.12

Let's write the desktop client application first. We will straight away write the code and not get into the Node.js setup, which we have already done in an earlier part of this chapter:

1. Create a file with the name `desktop_client.js` under any folder of your choice; just make sure you have Node.js and its modules installed there locally (refer to *Step 6* of the *HTTP server* section in this chapter).

2. Add the following code to include the (import) MQTT client module. You can check the link for more details about this module: `https://www.npmjs.com/package/mqtt`:

```
const mqtt = require('mqtt')
```

3. Provide connection details like port on which broker is running (default port: `1883`) and the public IP address of our server:

```
const options={
port:'1883',
host:'ip_address_of_broker_server'
}
```

4. Using the MQTT connect method, we will establish a connection with broker:

```
const client = mqtt.connect(options)
```

5. We will use the `client` object of the connect method to listen for a connect event, which gets fired on successful connection with the broker. As soon as we connect, we will subscribe to a topic as well, on which our Raspberry Pi client will publish. We also print to the console for our reference when we execute our code:

```
client.on('connect', () =>
{
client.subscribe('pub/data');
console.log("\r\n desktop mqtt client connected to broker
\r\n");
})
```

Here, the `pub/data` topic will be created when the Raspberry client publishes on it. Check the code section of the Raspberry client.

6. Once we subscribe to a topic, we listen for a `message` event of the `client` object to retrieve the actual data from the received message packet through a `callback` function. The `callback` function returns two values; one is the topic to which the `client` has subscribed and `data/message` received:

```
client.on('message', (topic, message) =>
{
    if (topic=='pub/data')
    {
        console.log('Data received from Rpi client on topic:
        pub/data '+ message.toString());
        client.publish('sub/ack','Ack: Success..!!');
        console.log("Acknowledgement sent to Rpi client ==>
        Ack: Success..!! \r\n")
    }
})
```

7. Using an `if` condition, we check whether we have received messages from the topic we have subscribed to. For our reference, we print the data received.

8. To send an acknowledgment, we publish a message on the topic `'sub/ack'`, which our Raspberry Pi client will subscribe to.

9. To check the successful implementation of our code, let's just run it using this command in the same sequence mentioned. Open the Command Prompt and move to the folder where we have our code file.

10. This will install the MQTT module:

    npm install mqtt --save

11. To execute the code run following command. On success, we will have output in our console as shown here:

    node desktop_client.js

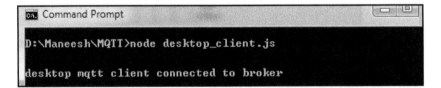

12. Now, we will create the Raspberry Pi client application.
13. Connect to the Pi using SSH/PuTTY, as shown in an earlier part of the chapter.
14. Create a file with the name `rpi_client.js`, using the nano editor, under any folder of your choice; just make sure you have Node.js and its modules installed there locally.
15. Execute this command to create and open the file in edit mode:

```
sudo nano rpi_client.js
```

16. Add this code to include/import the MQTT client module:

```
const mqtt = require('mqtt')
```

17. Provide connection details like port on which broker is running (default port: `1883`) and public IP address of our server:

```
const options={
 port:'1883',
 host:'ip_address_of_broker_server'
}
```

18. Using the MQTT connect method, we will establish a connection with the broker:

```
const client = mqtt.connect(options)
```

19. We will use the `client` object of the connect method to listen for a connect event, which gets fired on successful connection with the broker. As soon as we connect, we will subscribe to a topic on which will receive acknowledgment from our desktop client. We already defined the topic as `'sub/ack'` in the desktop client code:

```
client.on('connect', () => {
 console.log("Rpi mqtt client connected to brokerrn")
 client.subscribe('sub/ack')
})
```

20. Now, let's publish the data from the Raspberry client to the desktop client. This will publish the message `'pi_data'` every five seconds on the topic `'pub/data'`:

```
setInterval(function () {
 console.log('Data pushed from Pi client on topic: pub/data ==>
pi_data')
 client.publish('pub/data','pi_data')
},5000)
```

21. As we publish the data, listen for the `'message'` message of the `client` object to receive acknowledgement from the desktop client:

```
client.on('message', (topic, message) => {
 if (topic=='sub/ack'){
 console.log('Acknowledgement received on topic: '+topic+'
==>
 '+message.toString()+'rn')
 }
```

22. Using an `if` condition, we check whether we have received messages from the topic we have subscribed to, and for our reference, we print the data received from the desktop client.

23. To check the successful implementation of our code, let's just run it using the following command in the same sequence mentioned. Open the Command Prompt and move to the folder where we have our code file.

24. This will install the MQTT module:

```
sudo npm install mqtt -save
```

25. To execute the code run following command. On success, we will have output on our console as shown here:

```
sudo nano rpi_client.js
```

```
pi@raspberrypi:~/Node_Programs $ sudo node rpi_client.js
Rpi mqtt client connected to broker
```

26. Now, it is time to run both clients simultaneously and see the MQTT protocol working.

27. The Raspberry client publishes data every five seconds and receives an acknowledgment:

```
pi@raspberrypi:~/Node_Programs $ sudo node rpi_client.js
Rpi mqtt client connected to broker

Data pushed from Pi client on topic: pub/data ==> pi_data
Acknowledgement recieved on topic: sub/ack ==> Ack: Success..!!

Data pushed from Pi client on topic: pub/data ==> pi_data
Acknowledgement recieved on topic: sub/ack ==> Ack: Success..!!
```

28. The desktop client receives data every five second and sends an acknowledgement as a response:

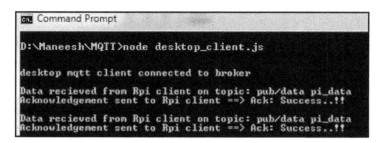

The following figure shows the architecture of our implementation of MQTT protocol:

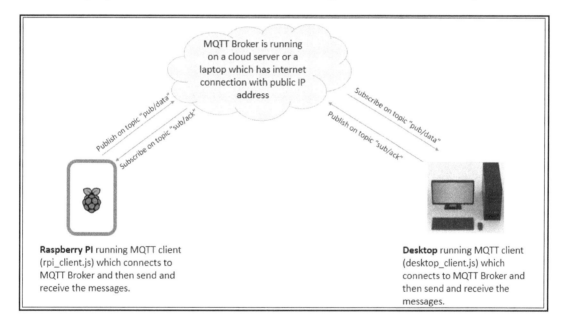

Summary

In this chapter, we learned about how the internet works; it is the backbone of communication. Why JavaScript and Node.js are becoming the favored choices for developing IoT applications. Then, we learned about HTTP and MQTT protocols thoroughly, implemented them using Raspberry Pi and servers, and demonstrated how communication happens between two machines.

In Chapter 4, *Weather Station*, we will build our first project, a weather station, using Raspberry Pi and multiple sensors.

4
Weather Station

In this chapter, we are going to build our first project, a weather station. Yes, you read it right, your own tiny weather station. You can place it inside or outside your house to measure the weather conditions. This IoT-based weather station will be equipped to measure temperature, humidity, wind speed, atmospheric pressure, sunrise, and sunset time. After collecting the weather data, we will push it to Google cloud spreadsheets, which you can access from anywhere in the world.

The weather station will have a digital temperature and humidity sensor, integrated with Raspberry Pi directly. For other parameters, such as wind speed, atmospheric pressure, and the time of sunset and sunrise, the data will be obtained from free and open source weather APIs, because sensors to measure such parameters are very expensive.

There will be four main components to our project:

- Sensors
- Weather APIs
- Raspberry Pi 3 Model B
- Google Sheets (cloud-based spreadsheets)

Let's go into the details of each component.

Sensors

As we learned in Chapter 2, *Know Your Raspberry Pi*, Raspberry Pi doesn't have analog inputs, so we will use digital sensors that are easy to use and low on cost as well.

Temperature sensor DS18B20

DS18B20 is a digital temperature sensor manufactured by the Dallas Semiconductor Company. It gives 9-to 12-bit temperature readings.

DS18B20 has three pins, **ground (GND)**, **Data line (DQ)**, and **power supply (VDD)**, as shown in the following diagram:

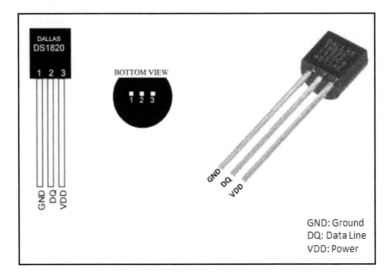

There is one more package available for these sensors, shown in the following figure, which is a waterproof version of DS18B20:

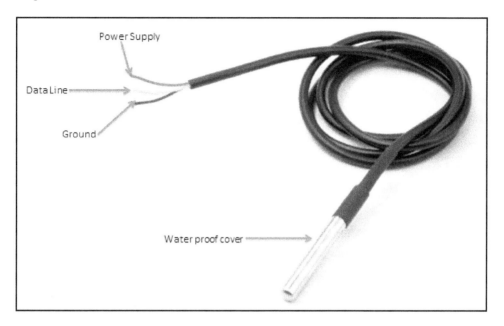

DS18B20 communicates with Raspberry Pi or any other controller device using the Dallas one-wire communication protocol. Raspberry Pi has provisions for sensors that communicate over the Dallas one-wire protocol, which makes the integration of this sensor pretty easy and straightforward.

The Dallas one-wire protocol is a serial communication method where data is transferred bit by bit over DQ. It is designed for simple communication between one master and multiple slave devices. In our case, Raspberry Pi is the master and the DS18B20 temperature sensor is the slave, which means we can integrate more than one temperature sensor on the same one-wire interface.

DS18B20 has a unique, factory-set, unchangeable device ID, using which each individual sensor can be identified over one-wire communication bus, as illustrated in the following figure:

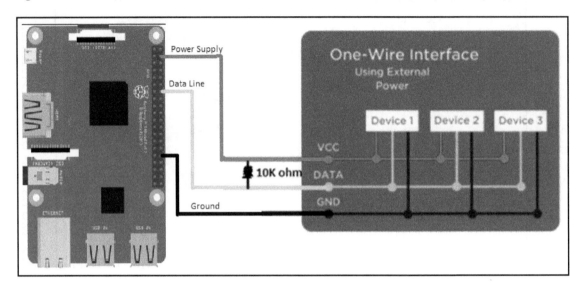

 The input power supply to the sensor should be between 3.3V and 5V DC only.

Due to this feature of interfacing multiple sensors on one data bus, DS18B20 is useful in applications such as HVAC environmental controls; sensing temperatures inside buildings, equipment, or machinery; and process monitoring and control where multiple sensors are required.

DHT11 humidity sensor

This is a digital humidity and temperature sensor combined together into one module. It is calibrated to provide digital signal output. The sensor package has a resistive humidity and NTC temperature measurement device that is connected to a high-performance 8-bit microcontroller with in the same package.

DHT11 has four pins, of which we will use three, namely power supply (3.3V to 5V DC), data line to read humidity data, and ground, as shown in the following figure:

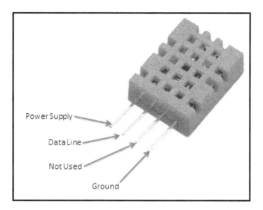

DHT11 uses a serial interface (single-wire bi-directional) for communication, which makes it extremely fast and responsive. Due to its low cost, low power consumption, strong anti-interference ability, precise calibration, and up to 20 m signal transmission, it's suitable for HVAC, consumer goods, the automotive industry, data logging, and weather stations.

Weather API

As we mentioned earlier, apart from temperature and humidity, we will measure wind speed, atmospheric pressure, and sunrise and sunset times using free and open source weather APIs.

Quite a few weather APIs are available for free. We will use the `OpenWeatherMap` API, which is easy to use and requires just a simple registration on their website to get started. It provides a REST-based API endpoint to get the weather data in JSON format. As input parameters, we need to provide a city ID, which is provided on the website itself, and APPID, which you will get after registration.

Let's go through the registration process and see how it works:

1. Log on to `http://www.openweathermap.com/` and click on **Sign Up**.
2. A registration page will appear; provide your username, email, and password to complete the registration.

3. Once successfully logged in to your account, the following page will appear:

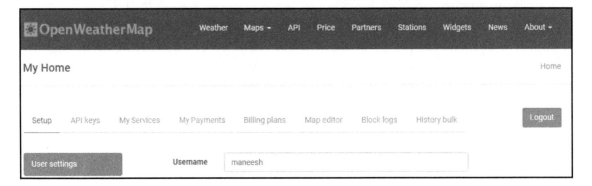

4. Select the **API keys** tab to get your key, which will be used in the API call:

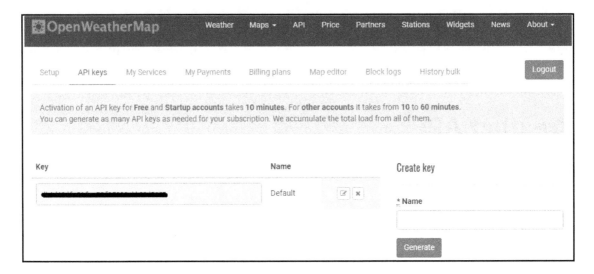

5. To get the IDs of your city and state, download the list (`city.list.json.gz`) from this link: `http://bulk.openweathermap.org/sample/`.

6. A brief description has been given on how to API endpoints at link: `https://openweathermap.org/appid`.

7. Try to get current weather data using the city ID and App key. We will use Postman as the API tool. You can use any API tool of your choice.

8. A HTTP `Get` request is sent along with `city id` and `APPID` (key), shown as follows:

- Request:

- Response:

```
{
    "coord": {
        "lon": 77.25,
        "lat": 28.78
    },
    "weather": [
        {
            "id": 711,
            "main": "Smoke",
            "description": "smoke",
            "icon": "50d"
        }
    ],
    "base": "stations",
    "main": {
        "temp": 283.15,
        "pressure": 1010,
        "humidity": 40,
        "temp_min": 283.15,
        "temp_max": 283.15
    },
    "visibility": 1500,
    "wind": {
        "speed": 2.6,
        "deg": 60
    },
    "clouds": {
        "all": 0
    },
    "dt": 1518230900,
    "sys": {
        "type": 1,
        "id": 7809,
        "message": 0.0074,
        "country": "IN",
        "sunrise": 1518228411,
        "sunset": 1518268137
    },
    "id": 1273293,
    "name": "National Capital Territory of Delhi",
    "cod": 200
}
```

In response, we get a long list of information but we will use wind speed, atmospheric pressure, and sunset and sunrise times. You can use other information as well if you want.

In our project, we will use this API endpoint programmatically in our code without using Postman.

Since we covered Raspberry Pi in depth in Chapter 2, *Know Your Raspberry Pi*, we are not going to cover it again here.

Google sheets

Google sheets is a cloud-based spreadsheet solution that is free to use; you just need a Google account for this. Google sheets provides APIs that let you read, write, and update your spreadsheets programmatically.

Let's dive into Google sheets and create one for our own use:

1. Log in to your Google account, or create one if you don't have an account already
2. Open the Google sheet by clicking on the icon that says **sheets**
3. This will redirect you to the Google sheets home page. Click on the plus icon to create a new/blank spreadsheet for our project
4. Once open, edit the name of the spreadsheet and change it to Weather Station
5. Since it autosaves, we don't need to worry about saving the spreadsheet after edits.

Now that we have created our spreadsheet, before we write the code and demonstrate the process of updating the spreadsheet using an API, we need to enable the API first.

 In case you need it, check out this link for more information on Google Sheets:
https://developers.google.com/sheets/api/quickstart/nodejs

Perform the following steps to enable it:

1. Enable the Google sheets API.
2. Navigate to https://console.developers.google.com/flows/enableapi? apiid=sheets.googleapis.com.

3. Select the **Create a project** option from the dropdown and click on **Agree and continue**:

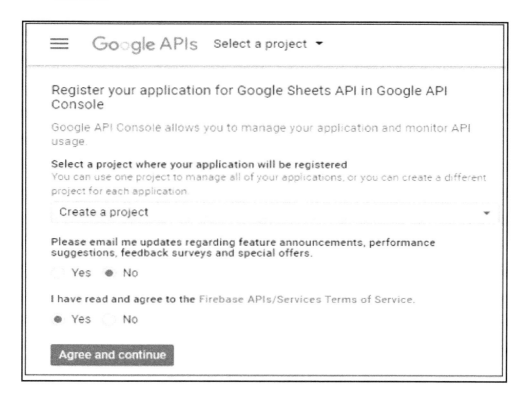

4. If the API is successfully enabled, you'll be presented with a success screen. Click on **Go to credentials** on the same screen:

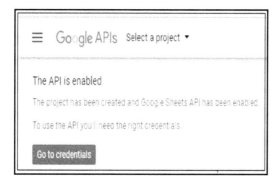

5. **Add credentials** to your project page will appear; click on **Cancel**.
6. At the top of the page, select the **OAuth consent screen** tab. Provide your **Email address**, give the product name as `WeatherStation`, and click on **Save**:

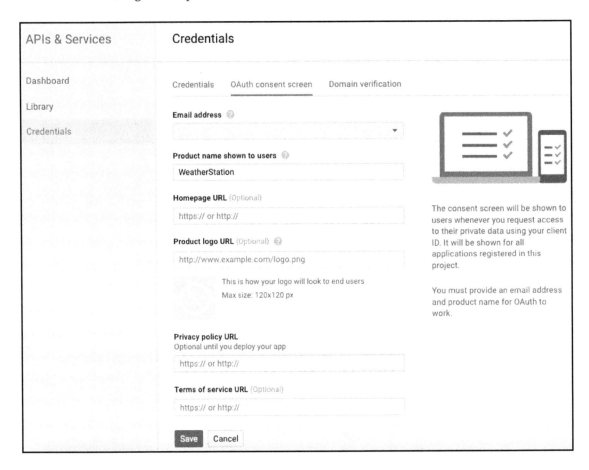

7. You will be routed to the credentials tab. Click on **Create credentials** and select **OAuth client ID**.

8. See the application type as **Other** and enter the name as `Google Sheet API`, as shown here:

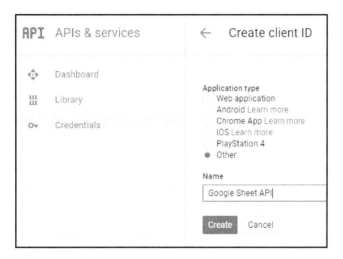

9. A popup will appear with the client ID and a secret key. Save it for later use. Click on **OK**.

10. Click on the **download** icon on the right to download the JSON file that will be used to access Google sheets programmatically:

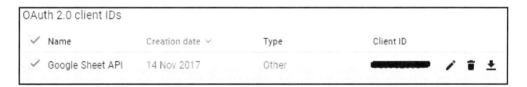

We have discussed all the components of our project in detail, now let's integrate all the pieces and build the weather station.

Let's interface the sensors first.

Whenever you're connecting anything to the GPIO pins on Raspberry Pi, make sure that your Pi is first turned off and unplugged from any power source.

For temperature sensor DS18B20, we are using the waterproof version of it. The following circuit diagram shows how to connect the sensors to Raspberry Pi:

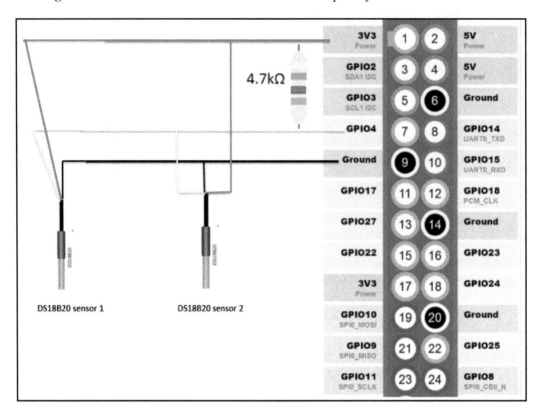

Let's review the circuit diagram. Raspberry Pi uses **GPIO 4** to communicate with temperature sensors over the one-wire protocol, so **GPIO 4** acts as a data line. We created a communication bus with the data line (**GPIO 4**) in yellow, the power line (3.3V) in red, and ground (GND) in black. Using this bus, we can interface multiple sensors simultaneously, as shown. A 4.7 k Ohm resistor is used between the data and power lines, which acts as pull-up resistor for the data line to keep the data transfer stable.

Now, we will interface the DHT11 humidity sensor with Raspberry Pi, as shown in the following diagram. Here, a **10 K Ohm** resistor is added between the power line (3.3V) and data line (**GPIO 27**), which acts as a pull-up resistor:

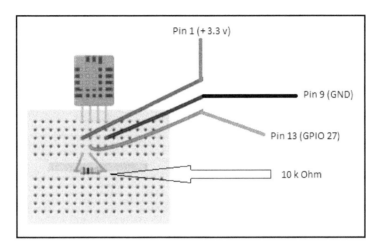

Since we have completed the circuit design part, now we will write the code for it. Our code will be divided into three major parts:

- Read data from the weather API
- Read data from sensors interfaced to Raspberry Pi
- Push all the data into Google Sheets

Let's write the code step by step.

Log in to Raspberry Pi and create and open a file with the name `weatherStation.js`, then include module request and request-promise:

```
var request = require('request');
var requestPromise = require('request-promise');
```

These modules are used to make HTTP requests to the `openweathermap` API, which we discussed earlier, to fetch weather data such as wind speed, air pressure, and sunset and sunrise times:

```
var options = { uri:
'http://api.openweathermap.org/data/2.5/weather?id=1273293&APPID=YOUR APP
ID/ APP KEY', };
```

The `options` contain the **Uniform Resource Identifier (URI)**, which is the API endpoint to get data from the `openweathermap` website. Two parameters are passed to the API endpoint: one is `id`, which indicates the city/state for which we want the weather data, and the other, `APPID`, is a key that is provided when we create an account on the `openweathermap` website, as described in an earlier section of this chapter.

The following piece of code will execute every five seconds with the help of the `setInterval` function. It will fetch weather data from the `openweathermap` API, fetch data from the temperature and humidity sensors, and update the Google spreadsheet:

```
var sensorData=require('./sensor');
var googleSheetAPI=require('./googlesheet');
 var sendInterval = setInterval(function () {
  var dataPacket= new Array(), arrayCounter=0;
  requestPromise(options)
    .then(function (response) {
      var APIresult=JSON.parse(response)
        dataPacket[arrayCounter]=APIresult.wind.speed;
        dataPacket[++arrayCounter]=APIresult.main.pressur;
        dataPacket[++arrayCounter]=APIresult.sys.sunrise;
        dataPacket[++arrayCounter]=APIresult.sys.sunset ;
    })
    .then(function(){
        sensorData.getSensorData(function(callback){
          var sensorDataResult=JSON.parse(callback);
  dataPacket[++arrayCounter]=sensorDataResult.temp_sens_1
  dataPacket[++arrayCounter]=sensorDataResult.temp_sens_2
  dataPacket[++arrayCounter] =sensorDataResult.humidity ;
console.log(dataPacket) ;

        })
    })
    .then(function(){
        googleSheetAPI.updateGoogleSheet(dataPacket)
      })
    .catch(function (err) {
      console.log(err);
  });
},5000)
```

Here, we have included the `sensor` and `googlesheet` modules at the top, which will give us access to the functions to get the data from the sensors and upload all the data to Google sheets.

Let's go through the preceding piece of code step by step and also write two other modules, `sensor` and `googlesheet`.

Using `setInterval`, we make sure that our code will get executed every defined interval of time; in our case, we have set the interval as 5 seconds, so the rest of the code is written inside the `setInrerval` function.

We declare an array with the name `dataPacket`, in which all the sensor and weather API data will be stored temporarily to be sent to Google sheets, and a counter, `arrayCounter`, is used to iterate over the array while inserting data into it.

We are using Node.js promises to make functions calls instead of `callback`, to avoid nested callback hell. We suggest you read about this separately.

Now, we make a call to the `openweathermap` API using `requestPromise` and passing `option` as the parameters that contain the `uri/api` endpoint. After a successful call, it returns a response, as shown in the following screenshot. Using the `then` functionality of the Node.js promise, we execute the next steps sequentially without getting into callback hell:

```
{
    "coord": {
        "lon": 77.25,
        "lat": 28.75
    },
    "weather": [
        {
            "id": 711,
            "main": "Smoke",
            "description": "smoke",
            "icon": "50d"
        }
    ],
    "base": "stations",
    "main": {
        "temp": 293.15,
        "pressure": 1018,
        "humidity": 40,
        "temp_min": 293.15,
        "temp_max": 293.15
    },
    "visibility": 1500,
    "wind": {
        "speed": 2.6,
        "deg": 50
    },
    "clouds": {
        "all": 0
    },
    "dt": 1518238800,
    "sys": {
        "type": 1,
        "id": 7809,
        "message": 0.0074,
        "country": "IN",
        "sunrise": 1518226411,
        "sunset": 1518266237
    },
    "id": 1273293,
    "name": "National Capital Territory of Delhi",
    "cod": 200
}
```

Since only a few data points are required, we parse the response as JSON and insert the data points into the array by iterating over it.

Again using the then function, we execute the next step to get the temperature and humidity sensor data interfaced to Raspberry Pi by calling the getSensorData function, itself provided by the sensor module, which has been included at the top. Now, let's create the sensor module and the getSensorData function in it.

Create a new file with the name sensor.js and include the following modules:

- onoff: It gives access to Raspberry Pi gpio
- fs: It enables us to read files
- rpi-dht-sensor: It enables us to read the humidity sensor data through Gpio:

```
var GPIO= require('onoff').Gpio,
fs= require('fs'),
rpiDhtSensor= require('rpi-dht-sensor');
```

For DS18B20 one-wire sensors, we need to configure Raspberry Pi by adding a few settings in the config.txt file under the /boot directory. For this, open the terminal and execute these commands:

```
cd /boot
sudo nano config.txt
```

This will open up the file, add the following lines to the file, and then close and save the file:

```
sudo modprobe w1-gpio
sudo modeprobe w1-therm
dtoverlay=w1-gpio
```

The DS18B20 temperature sensors are interacting with Raspberry Pi over one-wire protocol using the communication bus, as explained in the circuit diagram in an earlier section of this chapter. The data received over this bus from the one-wire sensors can be read from the file located at /sys/bus/w1/devices/. Under **devices**, each sensor will have a file with its unique serial number, starting with 28. Since the serial number, of one-wire sensors are factory-set, unchangeable, and unique, you can read them beforehand at /sys/bus/w1/devices/ by powering up Raspberry Pi after doing the preceding configuration and connecting the sensor to Raspberry Pi.

In our case, we have read the serial numbers of both sensors beforehand, so we are hardcoding their respective file paths to read the temperature data:

```
var device1_path='/sys/bus/w1/devices/28-0516a05186ff/';
var device2_path='/sys/bus/w1/devices/28-0517026efdff/'
```

The DHT11 humidity sensor is connected to GPIO 27, so declare this using the function provided by the rpi-dht-sensor module:

```
var dht=new rpiDhtSensor.DHT11(27);
```

Now, create a getSensorData function in which sensor data will be read and sent back to the calling function in the weatherStation.js file:

```
module.exports.getSensorData = function(callback){
    var readout=dht.read()
    var dht11_data=JSON.parse(JSON.stringify(readout)),
      dht11_data_humidity=dht11_data.humidity;
  var sensor1Data =fs.readFileSync(device1_path+'w1_slave');
sensor1Data=sensor1Data.toString().split('\n');
 var s1_line1Array=sensor1Data[0].split(' '),
 s1_line2Array=sensor1Data[1].split('t='),
 s1_raw_Temp=s1_line2Array[1],
 s1_temp_C=s1_raw_Temp/1000;
var sensor2Data =fs.readFileSync(device2_path+'w1_slave');
sensor2Data=sensor2Data.toString().split('\n');
var s2_line1Array=sensor2Data[0].split(' '),
 s2_line2Array=sensor2Data[1].split('t='),
 s2_raw_Temp=s2_line2Array[1],
 s2_temp_C=s2_raw_Temp/1000;
var sensordataPacket={
                "temp_sens_1": s1_temp_C,
                "temp_sens_2": s2_temp_C,
                "humidity": dht11_data_humidity
  }
sensordataPacket= JSON.stringify(sensordataPacket)
callback(sensordataPacket)
  }
```

We use modules.export to define this function in order to make it available in other modules. Inside the function, the DHT11 humidity sensor data is fetched using the read function provided by the rpi-dht-sensor module. After parsing, humidity data is stored in a variable for later use.

Then, we read out the temperature data for both the DS18B20 temperature sensor from its respective files located at their respective paths declared in the device_path1 and device_path2 variables, using the readFileSync function of the fs module.

The temperature data file looks as follows:

So to read the actual temperature data represented by t = XXXX in temperature data file, we do some string manipulation to convert it into an actual temperature reading in degrees Celsius. Repeat the same steps for the other temperature sensor.

A JSON object is created from the data of all three sensors and sends back to the calling function from the weatherStation.js module through callback. Once we receive the data, we insert each value into the dataPacket array by iterating over it as written in the weatherStation.js module.

Now we execute the final step, to update all the collected data in Google sheets. Make a call to the updateGoogleSheet function from the googlesheets module, which we included in weatherStation.js.

Let's write code for the googlesheets module. Create a new googlesheets.js file and include the required Google sheets modules:

```
var fs = require('fs');
var readline = require('readline');
var google = require('googleapis');
var googleAuth = require('google-auth-library');
```

Next we define the scope, which limits the kind of operation that we perform on Google sheets, such as read only and update only, but we keep our scope generic as we perform both read and write operations. Also, a security token will be generated and saved in the sheets.googleapis.com-nodejs-quickstart.json file when we execute the code for the first time. The path of this file will be stored in the TOKEN_PATH variable. This token will be used later to authenticate our read and write request:

```
var SCOPES = ['https://www.googleapis.com/auth/spreadsheets'];
var TOKEN_DIR = (process.env.HOME || process.env.HOMEPATH ||
```

```
                    process.env.USERPROFILE) + '/.credentials/';
                    console.log(TOKEN_DIR)
                    var TOKEN_PATH = TOKEN_DIR + 'sheets.googleapis.com-nodejs-
quickstart.json';
```

The `storeToken` function is used to store the token in the local disk:

```
function storeToken(token) {
  try {
    fs.mkdirSync(TOKEN_DIR);
  } catch (err) {
    if (err.code != 'EEXIST') {
      throw err;
        }
  }
  fs.writeFile(TOKEN_PATH, JSON.stringify(token));
  console.log('Token stored to ' + TOKEN_PATH);
}
```

When we execute the step to upload the data to Google sheets for the first time, a new token is generated by the `getNewToken` function and is stored on our local disk, using the `storeToken` function we just defined:

```
function getNewToken(oauth2Client, callback) {
  var authUrl = oauth2Client.generateAuthUrl({
    access_type: 'offline',
    scope: SCOPES
  });
  console.log('Authorize this app by visiting this url: ', authUrl);
  var rl = readline.createInterface({
    input: process.stdin,
    output: process.stdout
  });
  rl.question('Enter the code from that page here: ', function(code) {
    rl.close();
    oauth2Client.getToken(code, function(err, token) {
      if (err) {
        console.log('Error while trying to retrieve access token', err);
        return;
      }
      oauth2Client.credentials = token;
      storeToken(token);
      callback(oauth2Client);
    });
  });
}
```

We authorize our access to update Google sheets using the token generated through the `authorize` function:

```
function authorize(credentials, callback) {
  var clientSecret = credentials.installed.client_secret;
  var clientId = credentials.installed.client_id;
  var redirectUrl = credentials.installed.redirect_uris[0];
  var auth = new googleAuth();
  var oauth2Client = new auth.OAuth2(clientId, clientSecret, redirectUrl);
  // Check if we have previously stored a token.
  fs.readFile(TOKEN_PATH, function(err, token) {
    if (err) {
      getNewToken(oauth2Client, callback);
    } else {
      oauth2Client.credentials = JSON.parse(token);
      callback(oauth2Client);
    }
  });
}
```

Now, we write the `updateSheet` function, which will update the Google sheet with the data:

```
function updateSheet(auth){
 var sheets = google.sheets('v4');
  sheets.spreadsheets.values.append({
    auth: auth,
    spreadsheetId: 'YOUR SPREADSHEET ID',
    range: 'Sheet1!A2:B',
    valueInputOption: "USER_ENTERED",
    resource: {
      values: [dataArray ]
    }
  }, (err, response) => {
    if (err) {
      console.log('The API returned an error: ' + err);
      return;
    } else {
        console.log("Appended");
    }
  });
}
```

Finally, we create a `updateGoogleSheet` function, which will be accessed and called from the `WeatherStation.js` module. This function takes the client secret generated when the Google API was enabled, and uses it along with the token to complete the authorization, and then updates the Google sheet with the sensor and weather API data:

```
var dataArray= new Array();
module.exports.updateGoogleSheet= function(data){
    dataArray=data
    fs.readFile('client_secret.json', function processClientSecrets(err,
content) {
        if (err) {
          console.log('Error loading client secret file: ' + err);
          return;
        }
          authorize(JSON.parse(content), updateSheet);
    });
}
```

An array is declared, which will store the data packet passed as a parameter, by calling the function from the `weatherStation.js` module.

This completes the code part, so now let's execute `weatherStation.js`. Open the terminal and execute the following command:

```
sudo node weatheStation.js
```

It will prompt you with the following message:

```
Authorize this app by visiting this url:  https://accounts.google.com/o/oauth2/auth?access_type=offline&scope=https%3A%2F%2Fwww.googleapis
.com%2Fauth%2Fspreadsheets&response_type=code&client_id=152752360311-hsqtl0kf300c31rtio5c9k7boj9i8aku.apps.googleusercontent.com&redirect_
uri=urn%3Aietf%3Awg%3Aoauth%3A2.0%3Anoo
```

Copy the link into the browser and hit *Enter*. A page will come up and ask for permission; click on **ALLOW**, as shown in the following screenshot:

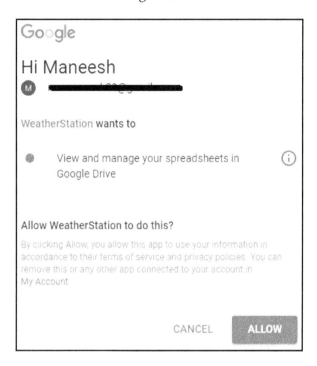

It will generate the code shown in the following screenshot:

Copy and paste it into the terminal and press *Enter*. On successful execution, you will see **appended** on the console, and the Google sheet will show the updated sensor and weather API data:

Wind Speed	Air Pressure	Sunrise Time	Sunset Time	Temp Sensor 1	Temp Sensor 2	humidity
3.6	1016	1514166108	1514203248	65.8616	66.9866	47
3.6	1016	1514166108	1514203248	65.8616	66.9866	47
3.6	1016	1514166108	1514203248	65.8616	66.9866	47
3.6	1016	1514166108	1514203248	65.8616	66.9866	47

Here is a flow diagram that will help us to understand the flow of execution of our code:

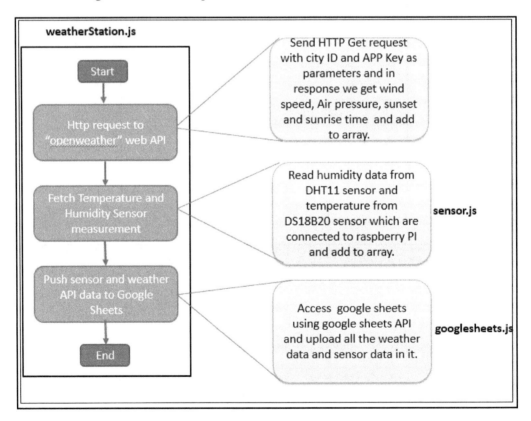

Summary

We have reached the end of this chapter, and achieved our target by building our own weather station. On this journey, we learned how to use weather APIs to collect data from the web based on location (city or state), then we learned about temperature and humidity sensors, and also integrated these with Raspberry Pi. Finally, we learned how to use Google sheets and how to update them programmatically.

Until now, we have only seen and learned how we can interface sensors to Raspberry Pi and send data from internet to server. In Chapter 5, *Controlling the Pi*, we will learn how we can control any device connected to raspberry remotely.

5
Controlling the Pi

Previously, we learned how to interface sensors with the Pi, which collects data and transmits it to a server/cloud over the internet. But in this chapter, we will learn how to communicate with the Pi in other ways, that is, to control the Raspberry Pi and devices/actuators connected to it remotely from the cloud over the internet.

As actuators or devices, we take a DC motor and a few LEDs that we want to control remotely.
The hardware requirements for this chapter will be:

- Raspberry Pi
- L293D motor driver IC
- DC motor
- Two LEDs

Since we have already been working with the Raspberry Pi and know it really well, we will focus on the details of the L293D motor driver, DC motor, and LED.

L293D

L293D is an integrated circuit chip most commonly used to drive the DC motor/stepper motor/gear motor. This IC consists of two H-bridges that can drive two DC motors simultaneously and in both clockwise and anticlockwise direction. It acts as an interface between the Raspberry Pi (or any other microprocessor) and the motor.

The DC motor needs a significant amount of current to start, which the Raspberry Pi is unable to provide as an output through GPIO. For example, a 5V DC motor needs around 300 to 400 mA current, which is way beyond what is available in the Raspberry Pi's GPIO, and if we directly connect the motor to the GPIO, it can damage the Pi. So, it is recommended you avoid directly connecting of the motor to Pi.

Let's look at the pin diagram for IC L293D to get an understanding of its operation:

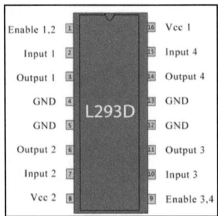

L293D has a 16-pin configuration. There are two Enable pins on the chip, pin 1 and pin 9; this **Enable** pin is used to drive the motor. If Enable is high, then the motor will run and if it is low, the motor will stop. Pins 4, 5, 12, and 13 are ground (**GND**).

There are four pins as Input, which decides the direction of the rotation of the motor; pins 2, 7, 10, and 14 are marked as input. These four input pins are used to drive two motors in a particular direction—two pins for each motor.

If **Input 1** (pin 2) is high and **Input 2** (pin 7) is low, the motor will rotate in a clockwise direction; if Input 1 (pin 2) is low and Input 2 (pin 7) is high, then the motor will rotate in an anti-clockwise direction. Similarly, for the other set of two pins, if **Input 3** (pin 10) is high and **Input 4** (pin 15) is low, the motor will rotate in a clockwise direction; if **Input 3** (pin 10) is low and **Input 4** (pin 15) is high, the motor will rotate in an anti-clockwise direction. The direction of rotation of motor also depends upon connection between motor terminal and output pins of L293D.

Four output pins are there to provide output to two motors. Pins 3 and 6 are connected to the two terminals of one motor, and pins 11 and 14 are connected to the terminals of other motor. Note that direction of motor rotation also depends upon connection between output pins and terminals of motor.

There are two Vcc pins—one is pin 8 (Vcc2), which is connected to a 9V/5V (voltage of battery depends upon the voltage rating of motor used) DC battery positive terminal. This Vcc2 is used for powering up the motor. The other one is pin 16 (Vcc1), used to power up L293D IC.

DC motor

A DC motor is an electric motor which converts electrical energy to mechanical energy. A DC motor works on a direct current and works on the principle that, when a current-carrying conductor is placed in a magnetic field, it experiences a torque and has the tendency to rotate. The direction of the current flowing in the conductor decides the direction rotation of the conductor.

We will not go into much detail about the internal workings of a DC motor, as this is beyond the scope of this chapter; I suggest you read more about it later.

For this chapter, we will use a 9V DC motor, as shown in the following diagram:

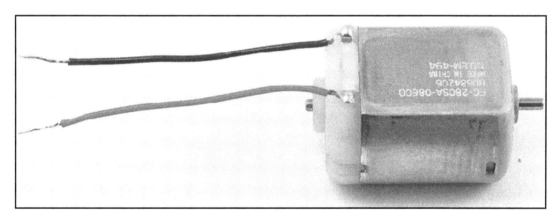

Light-emitting diode

A **Light-Emitting Diode** (**LED**) is a particular type of diode that converts electrical energy into light energy. An LED emits visible light when an electric current passes through it. LEDs are very efficient in operation, consume less power, and have a very long life. They are generally used in applications such as indicator lights, LCDs, remote controls, and many such electronic devices.

The following figure shows an LED and an internal circuit as well:

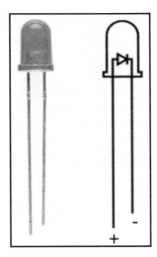

Since an LED is a diode, it allows current to flow only in one direction and, if the opposite polarity is applied it won't break—it just won't work. The positive side is called the anode (+) and the negative side is called the cathode (-). The current always flows from positive to negative. In an LED, the anode side lead/leg is always longer and is a good way to identify the anode and cathode.

We have covered all the components required to complete the project in this chapter; now let's integrate all the components together. Here, we will interface the LED and L293D to the Raspberry Pi directly and then interface the motor to the L293D.

Please follow the circuit diagram shown next:

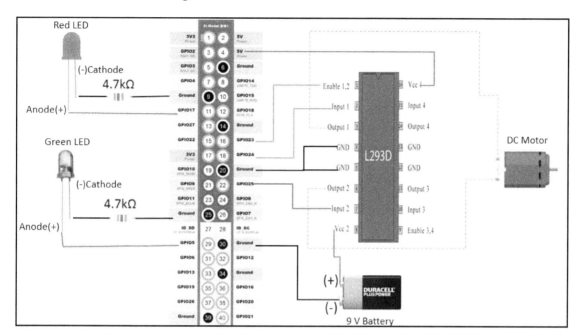

Connections shown in the figure are explained as follows:

- The **Red LED**'s positive terminal (+) is connected to GPIO 17 (pin 11) and the negative terminal (-) is connected to **Ground** (pin 9) with a 4.7 K Ohm resistor in series
- The **Green LED**'s positive terminal (+) is connected to GPIO 05 (pin 29) and the negative terminal (-) is connected to Ground (pin 25) with a 4.7 K Ohm resistor in series
- L293D's **Enable 1** (pin 1) is connected to GPIO 23 (pin 16)
- L293D's **Input 1** (pin 1) is connected to GPIO 24 (pin 18)
- L293D's **Input 2** (pin 7) is connected to GPIO 25 (pin 22)
- L293D's **Ground** (pins 4 and 5) are connected to the Raspberry Pi GND (pin 20)
- L293D's **Vcc 1** (pin 16) is connected to +5V (pin 04)
- L293D's **Vcc 2** (pin 8) is connected to the positive (+) terminal of the 9V battery

- The negative terminal of the 9V battery is connected to the **Ground** of the Raspberry Pi's pin 30
- L293D's **Output 1** (pin 3) is connected to one terminal of the motor
- L293D's **Output 2** (pin 6) is connected to another terminal of the motor

After completing the connections, we will write our code to complete the task. Basically, our code will allow us to start, stop, and rotate the motor in both directions (clockwise and anti-clockwise) remotely over the internet. When the motor rotates in a clockwise direction, the green LED will glow; when the motor rotates in an anti-clockwise direction the red LED will glow.

Let's write the code now. Here, we use the MQTT protocol to communicate with the Raspberry Pi from the server, which we have already learnt about in Chapter 3, *Let's Communicate*. We will not go into the details here again and directly implement it.

Take a server, which can be any Windows or Linux instance provided by AWS or Azure, and note its public IP address. The server can be your own laptop/desktop as well but it should be accessible over internet via its public IP address. Install the MQTT broker on this server and make sure it is up and running:

1. Log into the Raspberry Pi, create a directory, and install Node.js in it.
2. Now create a file with the name `Motor_LED.js` and include the `onoff` module, which will give you access to GPIO:

```
var GPIO= require('onoff').Gpio;
```

3. As per the circuit diagram in the previous figure, we need to set GPIO 17, 5, 23, 24, and 25 as the output pin:

```
var red_LED= new GPIO(17,'out'),
    green_LED= new GPIO(5,'out'),
    enable= new GPIO(23,'out'),
    input_1= new GPIO(24,'out'),
    input_2= new GPIO(25,'out');
```

4. While explaining L293D, we discussed the logic for clockwise and anti-clockwise rotation; now we write a function for it:

```
module.exports.rotate_clockwise = function(callback){
 enable.writeSync(1);
 input_1.writeSync(1);
 input_2.writeSync(0);
 green_LED.writeSync(1);
 red_LED.writeSync(0);
 console.log ("Clockwise Rotation")
callback("Clockwise Rotation")
}

module.exports.rotate_anti_clockwise = function(callback){
enable.writeSync(1);
 input_1.writeSync(0);
input_2.writeSync(1);
green_LED.writeSync(0);
red_LED.writeSync(1);

console.log ("Anti Clockwise Rotation")
callback ("Anti Clockwise Rotation")
}

module.exports.motor_stop = function(callback){
enable.writeSync(0);
input_1.writeSync(0);
input_2.writeSync(0);
green_LED.writeSync(0);
red_LED.writeSync(0);
console.log ("Motor Stopped")
callback ("Motor Stopped")
}
```

5. Now we will write a module for the Raspberry Pi that will connect to the MQTT broker to receive the command from the server in order to run the motor in either direction.

6. Create a new file in the same directory with the name `controlPi.js` and add the following code line. Here we include the `mqtt` module for connecting to MQTT server. Here we include the module `Motor_LED.js`, in which we have written motor rotation logic functions:

```
var mqtt = require('mqtt')
var motor_Dir= require('./Motor_LED');
```

7. `options` will have the IP address and port number to connect to the server, where we have the MQTT broker running:

```
var options = {
port:'1883',
host: "IP Address of Mqtt Broker server"
}
```

8. Now we listen on the `connect` event, which gets fired as soon as the connection to the MQTT broker is established. Once connected, we subscribe to the `controlPi/cmd` topic as we send the control signal from `mqtt client` to this topic. We receive all the control commands for the LED and motor operation on the topic `controlPi/cmd`:

```
var client = mqtt.connect(options)
client.on('connect', () => {
client.subscribe('controlPi/cmd');
console.log ("\r\n Raspberry Pi mqtt client connected to broker
\r\n ");
})
```

Now we listen to the event `message` which occurs whenever a message/data is received on a subscribed topic. Once the message is received, we call the appropriate function for rotating the motor clockwise and anti-clockwise and send the acknowledgment to the client using the `publish` method of `mqtt`:

9. The acknowledgment is sent from the Raspberry Pi on the topic `raspbPi/ack`, which is subscribed by the client:

```
client.on ('message', (topic, message) => {
   message= message.toString();
   if(message=='clockwise') {
     motor_Dir.rotate_clockwise((callback) => {
     var Acknowledgement=callback;
     client.publish ('raspbPi/ack', Acknowledgement);
   });
}
else if(message=='anticlockwise') {
motor_Dir.rotate_anti_clockwise((callback) => {
var Acknowledgement=callback;
client.publish('raspbPi/ack',Acknowledgement)
 });
}
else {
motor_Dir.motor_stop((callbacka)=> {
```

```
var Acknowledgement=callback;
client.publish('raspbPi/ack',Acknowledgement)
})
}
})
```

10. Now let's run the code. Open Terminal and execute the following command:

    sudo node controlPi.js

11. On successful execution, the Raspberry Pi will connect to the MQTT broker and a message will come up on the console, as shown in the following screenshot:

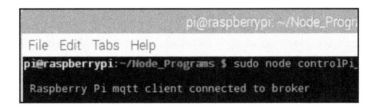

Now the Raspberry Pi is connected to the MQTT broker and subscribed the topic `controlPi/cmd`.

Here, we will use an open source `mqtt client` on our laptop/desktop to send the control commands for operating the motor interfaced with the Raspberry Pi in a clockwise and anti-clockwise direction:

1. For this purpose, we download the `mqtt.fx` (`http://mqttfx.jensd.de/`) client tool and make a connection to the MQTT broker running on the server, as shown in the following screenshot.

2. Provide the MQTT broker details and connect. The **Edit Connection Profiles** window will pop up after you click on the **Settings** button, adjacent to the **Connect** button:

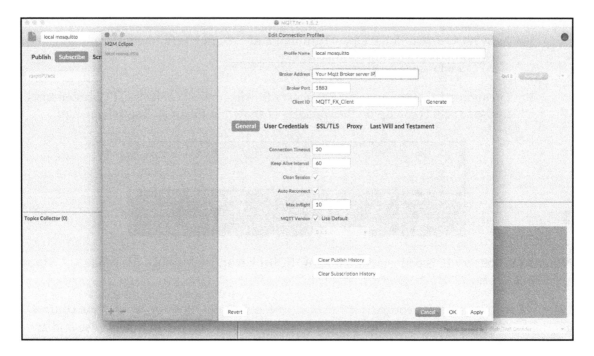

3. Once successfully connected to the broker, a green signal appears in the top-right corner of the mqtt.fx window, as shown here:

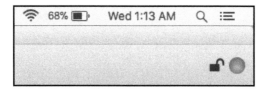

4. We need to subscribe to the topic `raspbPi/ack` from `mqtt.fx`, on which a acknowledgement from the Pi will be received, as shown next:

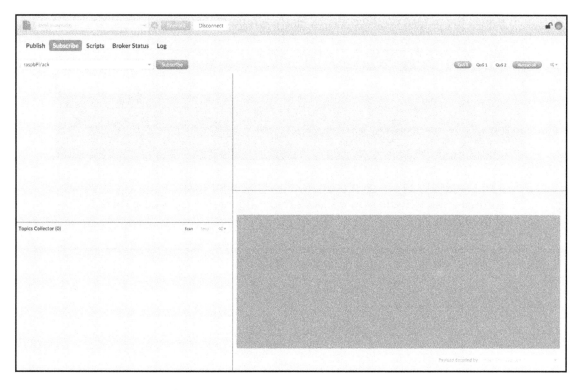

5. Now both the Raspberry Pi and the `mqtt.fx` client are connected to the MQTT broker which is running on the cloud/server, so let's play the game.

6. **Publish** a message `clockwise` on the topic `controlPi/cmd` from the `mqtt.fx` client, as shown here:

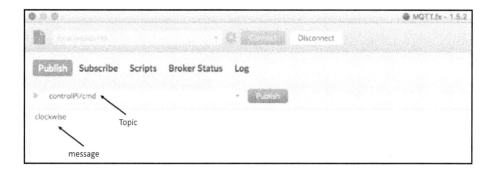

7. Since `mqtt client` on the Raspberry Pi has already subscribed to the same topic, it receives the message and, as per the logic written in the code, it will start rotating the motor in a clockwise direction and switch on the green LED. Also notice the output on the console, as shown here:

8. The Raspberry Pi also sends an acknowledgment to the `mqtt.fx` client as a confirmation that the motor has started moving in a clockwise direction, as shown here:

9. Similarly, we send a command to rotate the motor in an **anticlockwise** direction, as shown next:

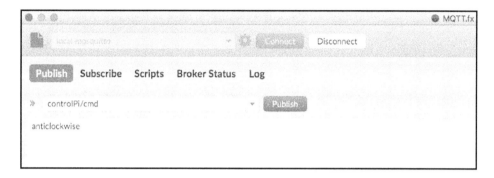

10. The motor will start moving in an anticlockwise direction and a red LED will glow. An acknowledgement of this will also be received, as shown next:

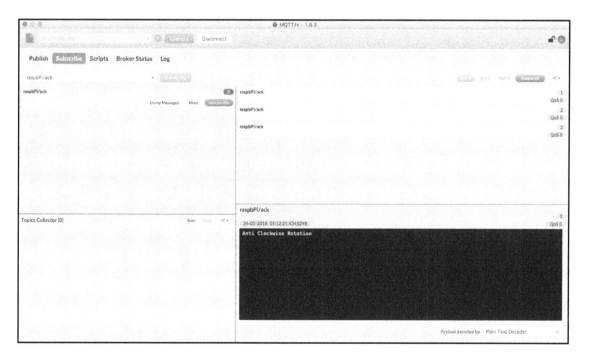

11. To stop the motor, we will send a `stop` message, as shown next:

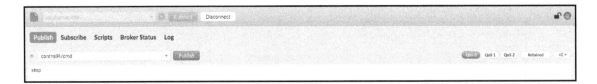

12. The motor stops and both LEDs will be switched off. An acknowledgment of this is also received, as shown here:

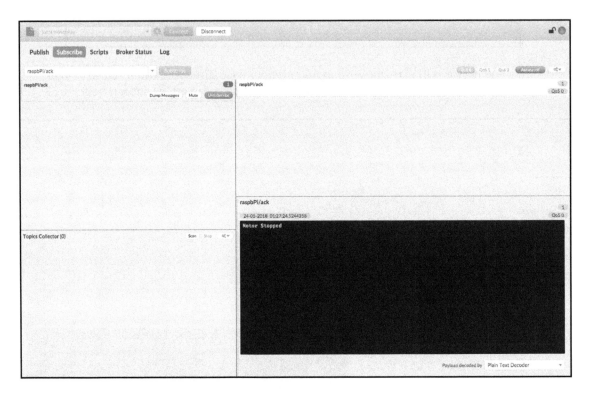

13. Let's look at the architecture of our solution, which will further clarify what we have done in this chapter; it is shown in the following figure:

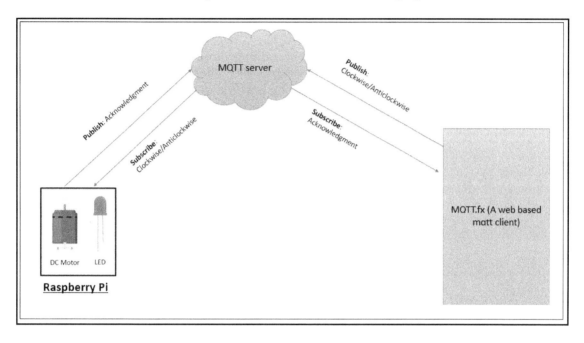

14. Now we will look at a diagram showing the execution of our code, which will help us grasp the whole logic; it is shown in the following figure:

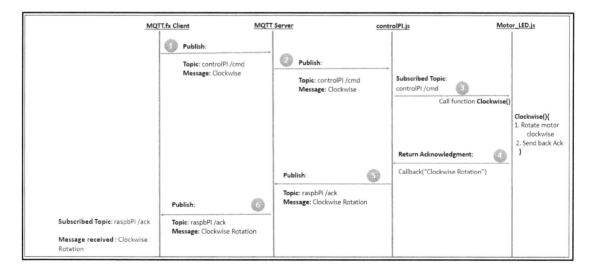

Summary

In this chapter, we learned about DC motors, LEDs, the L293D motor driver IC, and the mqtt.fx web client.

We interfaced LED to the Raspberry Pi directly and interfaced the DC motor to the Raspberry Pi with the help of the L293D motor driver IC. Then, by implementing the MQTT protocol for communication, we controlled the motion and direction of the motor rotation using the mqtt.fx web client. We have achieved our goal and successfully have controlled the motor and LEDs interfaced with the Raspberry Pi remotely over the internet.

In Chapter 6, *Security Surveillance*, we will build next project which is a security surveillance system to protect your home/premises from intruders. We will use Raspberry Pi, camera module, and motion sensor to complete this project.

6
Security Surveillance

Are you worried about security of your home in your absence? Then you need not worry at all because you can build your own security surveillance system in no time.

So, let's build a security surveillance system that will keep an eye on your home, shops, offices, garage, or any other property in your absence. If someone trespasses on your property, it will raise an alarm, take photographs and a video recording of the trespassers, and send them to you over email.

In this chapter, we will learn about the following modules, which are used to build the system:

- Infrared sensors
- Ultrasonic sensor
- Alarm/buzzer
- LED
- Raspberry Pi camera module
- Raspberry Pi 3

Infrared sensors

First, let's understand what **Infrared Radiation** (**IR**)? Infrared is a region of the electromagnetic radiation spectrum, where the wavelength is between 700 nm to 1 mm, which is more than the wavelength of visible light and less than radio waves. The frequency of IR is in the range of 300 GHz to 400 GHz, which is higher than the frequency of microwaves, but lower than that of visible light.

IR waves are not visible to human eye unlike visible light, but can be focused, reflected, and polarized just like visible light.

IR is mostly used in wireless communication, remote controls, sensors, thermal imaging, and night vision devices, but we will focus only on IR sensors in this chapter.

IR sensors are the devices that emit or/and detect IR radiation. The working principle of any IR sensor is governed by Plank's radiation law. As per Plank's radiation law, any object that has a temperature not equal to absolute zero (which is **zero kelvin ($0°$ K)**) emits radiation.

In our case, we use IR sensors for obstacle or object detection, and for these applications the IR sensor module should consist of the following components:

- **IR transmitter**: An IR transmitter is a source of IR radiation for which IR LEDs and lasers are used.
- **Transmission medium**: For the transmission of IR waves, a medium such as a vacuum, atmosphere, or optical fibers is required.
- **Optical component**: Materials such as quartz are used to focus the infrared radiation in a particular area. Optical lenses such as quartz, germanium, and silicon are used to make optical components.
- **IR receiver/detector**: Photodiodes and LED are used as IR receivers and detectors respectively, which have good photo sensitivity for infrared radiations.
- **A signal processing module**: A signal processing module is used to amplify the signal received by the IR detector because the amplitude of the signal is very small.

Types of IR sensors

There are basically two types of IR sensor: Passive IR sensors and Active IR sensors.

Passive Infrared Sensors (**PIR sensors**) do not need an infrared source to operate. PIR sensors detect the infrared rays emitted. The main application of these motion detection sensors is to the check the presence of any human or animal since the body of a human and animal radiates infrared energy.

Let's understand the anatomy of the PIR sensor module that we will be using to build our surveillance system. We use the readily available HC-SR501 PIR Sensor module. Refer to *Figure 6.1*:

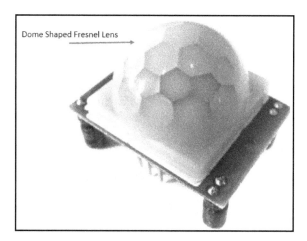

Figure 6.1

The preceding picture shows the top view of the PIR module with a dome-shaped fresnel lens mounted on it. This lens helps to focus infrared radiation.

Inside this fresnel lens, there is a pyroelectric sensor, which detects the IR radiation; refer to *Figure 6.2*, which shows a picture of the pyroelectric sensor enclosed in a metal body with a rectangular crystal in the center:

Figure 6.2

Along with the pyroelectric sensor, supporting circuitry is situated on the other side of the module, as shown in *Figure 6.3*:

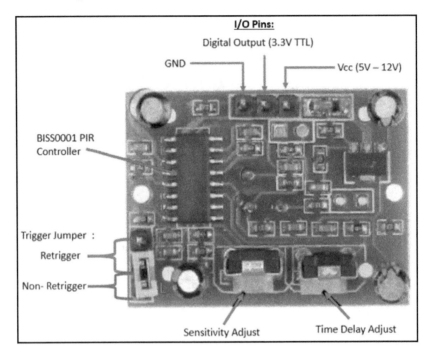

Figure 6.3

The supporting circuitry has a few important components that play a major role in the operation of the PIR sensor module:

- **I/O pins**:
  - The first pin is for powering the sensor itself, marked as Vcc. The PIR sensor has an operating range of 5V to 12V.
  - The second pin reads the output of the PIR sensor, marked as 3.3V TTL. It generates a digital output, which goes high when the sensor detects infrared radiation and goes low when there is no radiation in its range.
  - The third pin is for grounding the sensor module marked as GND.

- **B1SS0001 PIR controller IC**:
    - A CMOS-based chip designed specifically for human-infrared sensor control circuits
    - Low power consumption and suitable for battery-powered operations
    - High input impedance operational amplifier
    - Bi-directional level detector/excellent noise immunity
    - Built-in power up disable and output pulse control logic
    - Dual operating modes: retriggerable and nonretriggerable
- Trigger settings include three pins and at any time only two pins are shorted using the jumper. When the pin marked **H** (refer to *Figure 6.3*) is shorted with the middle pin, the sensor works in retrigger mode. In retrigger mode, the PIR sensor gives continuous high output for a certain duration of time when it detects any human body (infrared radiation is emitted from the human body due to body heat). And when the pin marked as **L** (refer to *Figure 6.3*) is shorted with the middle pin, the sensor works in nonretrigger mode. In nonretrigger mode, the PIR sensor's output keeps on switching between high and low when it detects any human body.

    For our use case, we will set the Trigger in retrigger mode by shorting pin **H** with the middle pin:

- Sensitivity of the PIR sensor can be altered using the **Trimpot** provided on the module and marked as **Sensitivity Adjust** (refer to *Figure 6.3*). When the **Trimpot** is turned in a clockwise direction, the sensitivity is increased and it detects even the slightest movement of a human body (a source of infrared radiation) from a distance of 6 meters or more approximately. And when it is turned in an anticlockwise direction, the sensitivity is decreased and it detects motion within a small range of 2 to 3 meters.

- **Delay time** determines how long the PIR sensor's output will remain high after detecting the motion. A **Trimpot** marked as **time delay Adjust** is provided to vary the delay time. The time value can be set from a few seconds to few minutes. When the **Trimpot** is turned in a clockwise direction, the delay time increases and the output will remain high for a longer period; when it's turned anticlockwise, the delay time reduces.

Until now, we have discussed the anatomy of the PIR sensor module. Let's understand how the PIR sensor actually works. A PIR sensor has two slots and each slot detects infrared radiation separately as shown in *Figure 6.4*. Here, each slot is made up of IR-sensitive material:

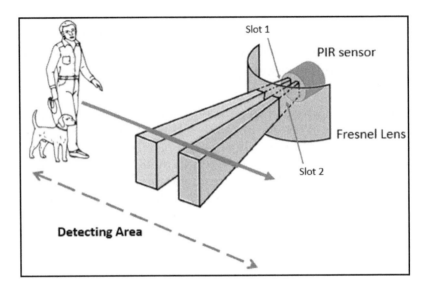

Figure 6.4

When there is no movement in front of the sensor, it remains in the idle state and both **Slot 1** and **Slot 2** detect the same amount of infrared radiation. When a warm body like that of a human or an animal passes by the detecting area, the IR radiation from the body is first detected by **Slot 1** of the PIR sensor, which results in a positive differential change between two slots. And when the body leaves the detecting area, the IR radiation is detected by **Slot 2**, which results in a negative differential change between the two slots. The combination of this positive and negative differential change results in the output signal at the PIR sensor, which is being read out through I/O pins.

Active infrared sensor modules consist of two elements: An infrared source and infrared detector. A source can be an LED or laser diode whereas an infrared detector can be a photodiode or phototransistor. When Energy (IR radiation) emitted by the source is reflected from any object and falls on the detector, it generates a signal. A typical setup of an IR object detector module can be seen in *Figure 6.5*:

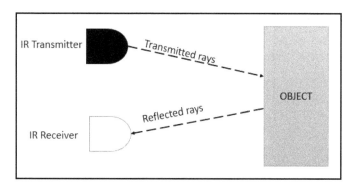

Figure 6.5

In our use case, the IR transmitter is an LED (refer to *Figure 6.6*), which emits infrared radiation. It looks like a normal LED, but the light emitted by it is not visible to the naked human eye:

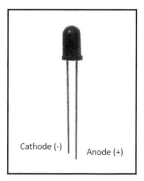

Figure 6.6

The IR receiver detects the radiation emitted by the transmitter. In our use case, we use an infrared photodiode as the IR receiver (refer to *Figure 6.7*). The IR photodiode is different from the normal photodiode because it only detects infrared radiations:

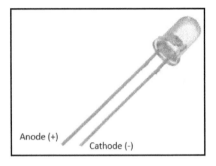

Figure 6.7

Note that, when an IR photodiode is used in conjunction with an IR transmitter in an object detection circuit, then the wavelength of both the transmitter and receiver should match.

Let's look at the IR sensor module that we are going to use to build our surveillance system (refer to *Figure 6.8*):

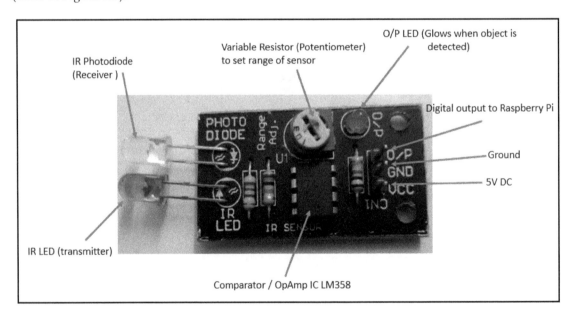

Figure 6.8

The following are the ingredients of the IR module:

- LM358
- IR transmitter and receiver pair
- Potentiometer: 10 k
- LED
- 270 Ohm resistor X 2
- 10 Ohm resistor

Let's explain the working of the IR module with the help of its circuit diagram shown in *Figure 6.9*:

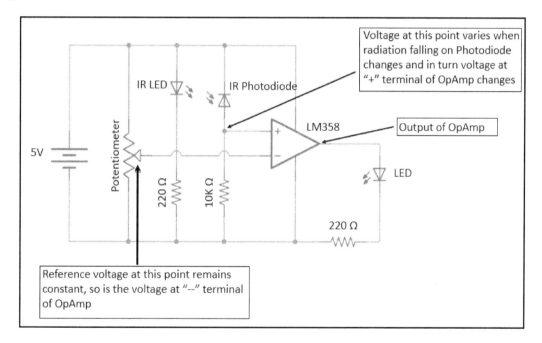

Figure 6.9

When an object comes close to an IR LED, infrared rays get reflected from the object and fall on an IR photodiode (receiver), which causes current to flow in the circuit. The energy from the IR waves is absorbed by electrons at the p-n junction of the IR photodiode, which causes the current flow.

When the current flows through a 10 k Ohm resistor, it creates a potential difference (voltage). This voltage value depends upon Ohm's law ($V=IR$). Since resistance is constant, the current, more will be the higher the voltage. The amount of current flow is directly proportional to the infrared waves detected by the photodiode. In simpler words, greater the intensity of the IR waves received by photodiode (the closer the object, the greater the quantity of reflected IR waves), the more current will flow through it and the higher the voltage.

The voltage output generated by the sensor is compared with a fixed value of reference voltage using LM358 opAmp IC (the reference voltage is created using a potentiometer). As shown in *Figure 6.9*, the positive terminal (non-inverting) of the OpAmp is connected to the positive terminal of photodiode (the voltage at this point changes when the object moves across the photodiode) and the negative (inverting) terminal of the OpAmp is connected to the reference voltage point (it remains constant) across the potentiometer.

The OpAmp works in such a way that when the voltage at the positive terminal of the OpAmp is more than that of the voltage at the negative terminal, the OpAmp generates an output, which eventually turns on the LED.

So, in a nutshell, when an object moves closer to the IR sensor, the IR waves that get reflected from it fall on the IR photodiode, which causes the voltage at the positive terminal of the OpAmp to increase; at a certain point it becomes more than reference voltage at a negative terminal and we get the output, which can be used to raise an alert by powering a buzzer or blinking an LED.

The sensitivity (minimum distance at which the sensor detects an object) can be altered by rotating the potentiometer.

Ultrasonic sensors

Ultrasonic sensors are used for noncontact proximity, object detection, and distance measurement. As the name suggests, these sensors use ultrasonic waves as a source to detect the object and its distance. The sensor measures the distance to an object by calculating the time between emission and reception of ultrasonic waves. Ultrasonic waves are very accurate over a short distance and do not create disturbances as they are inaudible to human ears.

The sensor has both an ultrasonic transmitter and receiver. The sensor works on the same principle as that of sonar/radar, which evaluates the presence of an object by listening to the echo of sound waves or radio waves reflected from the object. The sensor emits a burst of high frequency, short-wavelength ultrasonic rays, which when echoed back from the object are received at the sensor. The time difference between sending and receiving the echo is used to calculate the distance of the object from the source (sensor). Refer to *Figure 6.10* to understand the basic setup and working of an ultrasonic sensor:

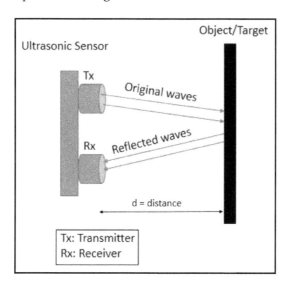

Figure 6.10

In our use case, we make use of the readily available ultrasonic sensor module HC-SR04, as shown in *Figure 6.11*:

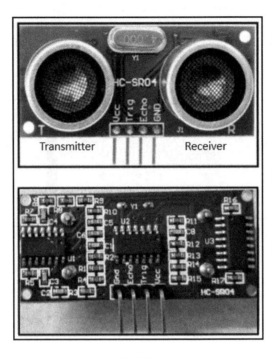

Figure 6.11

As shown in the preceding figure, the HC-SR04 ultrasonic sensor module has four pin outs, which are explained as follows:

- **Vcc**: Here we apply a 5V input voltage that will power the sensor.
- **Trig**: A high signal (3.3V TTL) is applied at **Trig**, which will cause the sensor to emit high-frequency ultrasonic waves.
- **Echo**: At this terminal, we read the output of the sensor. When we apply the high signal at pin **Trig**, the ultrasonic waves are emitted from the transmitter and the **Echo** pin goes high and remains high until we receive the ultrasonic waves at the receiver, which is reflected/echoed back after bouncing off from an object/obstruction.
- **GND**: This pin is used to ground the sensor.

Let's understand the workings of the ultrasonic sensor in more detail with the help of a timing diagram as shown in *Figure 6.12*:

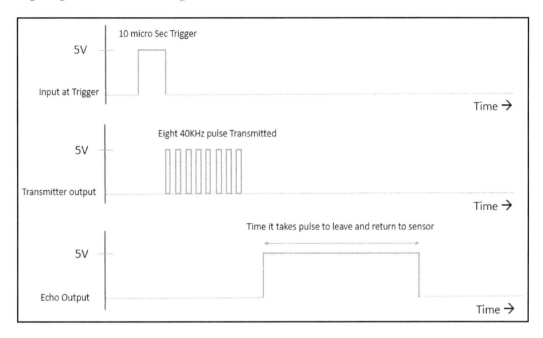

Figure 6.12

When we apply a high signal for 10 microseconds on the **Trigger** (**Trig Pin**), it causes the transmitter to emit a burst of eight high-frequency (40 KHz) pulses of ultrasonic waves. The output at the **Echo** pin goes high and when the ultrasonic waves return to the receiver of the sensor, the output at the **Echo** pin goes low again. We log the time stamps when the output at the **Echo** pins go from low to high and high to low and calculate the difference between both timestamps. This time difference is proportional to the distance between the sensor and object from which the ultrasonic waves are reflected back.

Let's calculate the exact distance of the object from the sensor using the following formula:

$$\text{Speed} = \frac{\text{Distance}}{\text{Time}}$$

The speed of sound waves (ultrasonic) = 330 m/s.

The distance traveled by *waves* = 2 x d. The total distance traveled by waves is twice the distance between the sensor and the object because waves travel twice—once when transmitted from the sensor and next when reflected from the object (refer to *Figure 6.10*):

Time = (time at which the ultrasonic waves are received - the start time of the ultrasonic waves)

By using the preceding formula and information, we can easily calculate the value of *d* (distance). In our use case, we are building a security surveillance system, where we can put this sensor at different places such as gates and lockers and we can design the rest of the circuit in such a way that, when any person or object comes within certain distance of the gate or locker, then it can raise an alarm.

Buzzer

We use a buzzer that is an important component of our surveillance system. In the event a trespasser bypasses the manual security, our surveillance system will not miss the trespasser. When detected near the restricted area, an alarm is raised with the help of the buzzer, which will alert the security people and force the trespasser to run away.

We make use of a piezo buzzer, which is readily available and cost-effective. A piezo buzzer is built of a piezo-electric material. The working of the piezo buzzer is based on the inverse of the principle of piezo electricity. The principle of piezo electricity states that whenever mechanical pressure is applied on piezo electric material, it generates electricity. And piezo buzzers follow the opposite principle, which states that when a voltage is applied on a piezo electric element, it deforms back and forth (a change in dimension takes place) and produces an audible sound.

Figure 6.13 shows a piezo electric buzzer:

Figure 6.13

We are using a LED as an indicator. Since we have already discussed LED in detail in `Chapter 5`, *Controlling the Pi*, we will not go through it again.

Raspberry Pi camera module

Any security surveillance system is incomplete without the digital eyes of a **camera**. With the use of a camera, we can keep a real-time watch at our place or premises even when we are not present. If any trespasser enters our premises, then with a combination of sensors and camera, we can make a video recording or take pictures, which can help to track down the trespasser later on.

In our use case, we will use the Raspberry Pi camera module, which is an add-on accessory provided by the Raspberry Pi foundation itself, as shown in *Figure 6.14*:

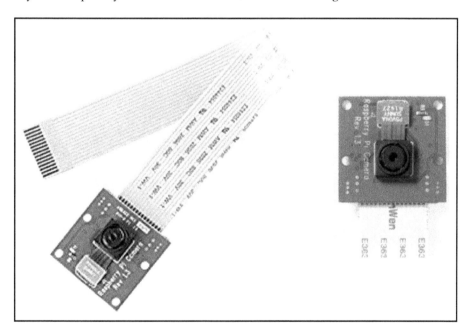

Figure 6.14

This camera module can be easily interfaced with the Raspberry Pi's dedicated CSI camera port. This camera has a ribbon cable that attaches the camera to Pi. Refer to the official video by the Raspberry Pi foundation to install the camera on the Pi correctly. The following is the video link: `https://www.raspberrypi.org/documentation/usage/camera/README.md`.

We have learned about each and every component required to build the security surveillance system except the Raspberry Pi itself, which is the heart of the system. But we will not go into the details, as we have been using it throughout the book. However, if you think you need to brush up your knowledge, I suggest you to go through `Chapter 2`, *Know Your Raspberry Pi*, and then come back and continue from here.

Wiring up

So far, we have discussed all the components of our system in detail and now we will wire up all the components together with the Raspberry Pi, one by one.

Interfacing PIR sensor module HC-SR501

Refer to *Figure 6.15* for connection details:

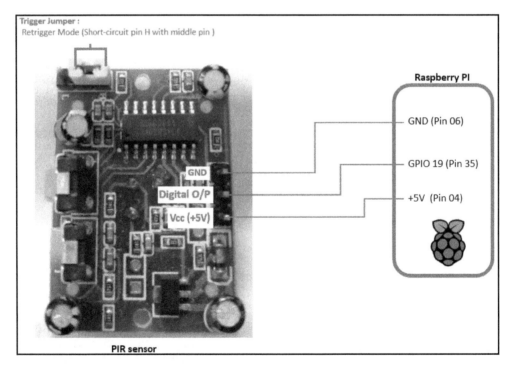

Figure 6.15

As shown in *Figure 6.15*:

- The ground terminal of the PIR sensor is connected to the ground pin of the Raspberry Pi **GND (Pin 06)**
- The output of the sensor is connected to **GPIO 19 (pin 35)** of the Raspberry Pi
- The **Vcc** terminal is connected to **+5V (pin 04)** of Raspberry Pi

Interfacing an active IR sensor

Refer to *Figure 6.16* for connection details:

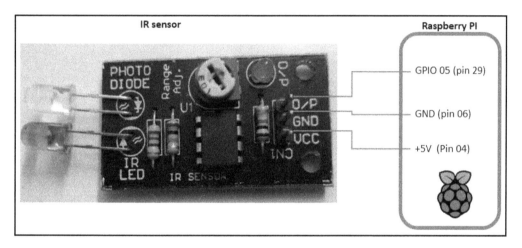

Figure 6.16

In *Figure 6.16*:

- The **O/P** terminal of the sensor is connected to **GPIO 05 (pin 29)** of Raspberry Pi
- The **GND** terminal of the sensor is connected to **GND (pin 06)** of Raspberry Pi
- The **Vcc** terminal of the sensor is connected to **+5V (pin 04)** of Raspberry Pi

Interfacing an ultrasonic sensor HC-SR04

Refer to *Figure 6.17* for connection details:

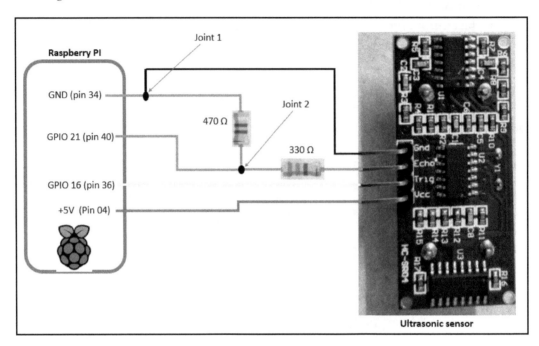

Figure 6.17

As shown in *Figure 6.17*:

- The **Gnd** terminal of the sensor is connected to **GND (pin 34)** of Raspberry Pi
- The **Echo** terminal of the sensor is connected to **GPIO 21 (pin 40)** of Raspberry Pi with a **330 Ω** resistor in between
- One more connection is taken out from the **Echo** terminal with a **470 Ω** resistor in between, from a point marked as **Joint 2**, and connected to the GND terminal of Raspberry Pi through **Joint 1**
- The **Trig** terminal of the sensor is connected to **GPIO 16 (pin 36)** of Raspberry Pi
- The **Vcc** terminal of the sensor is connected to **+5V (pin 04)** of Raspberry Pi

Interfacing an LED

Refer to *Figure 6.18* for connection details:

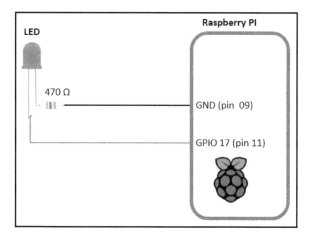

Figure 6.18

As shown in *Figure 6.18*:

- The positive terminal (the longer leg) of **LED** is connected to **GPIO 17 (pin 11)** of Raspberry Pi
- The negative terminal (the shorter leg) of **LED** is connected to **GND (pin 09)** of Raspberry Pi

Since we have already installed the camera module in Raspberry Pi, let's enable it in Raspberry Pi configurations before we write the code.

If you have connected your pi with the monitor using HDMI or VGA, then you can log into it and go to **Menu | Preference | Raspberry Pi Configuration**, as shown in *Figure 6.19*:

Figure 6.19

Under **Raspberry Pi Configuration**, go to the **Interfaces** tab and enable the **Camera**, as shown in *Figure 6.20*:

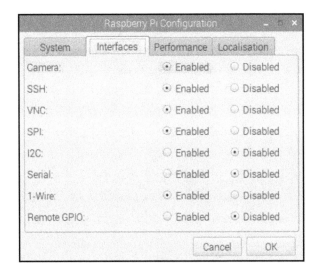

Figure 6.20

If you do not have a separate monitor to connect to Raspberry Pi, with the help of headless setup (refer to `Chapter 2`, *Know Your Raspberry Pi*, for details about headless setup), you can then connect to Raspberry Pi using PuTTy, as shown in *Figure 6.21*:

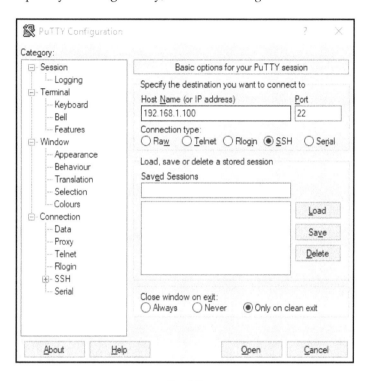

Figure 6.21

Once logged in using the username and password, run the `raspi-config` in Terminal, which will open up the configuration window as shown in *Figure 6.22*. Select the **Enable Camera** option and then click on **Finish**. This will enable the camera and now we are good to go and write our code:

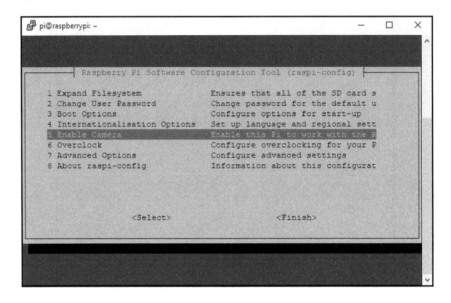

Figure 6.22

The code

Let's write the code to bring our surveillance system to life.

The setup requires Node.js to be installed on Raspberry Pi which we have already done quite a few times through out this book so we will not repeat that and straightaway start writing the code.

Camera module code

To use the camera, we need to include a library from npm. We use the pi-camera library, and to install it, run the command in the terminal, as shown in *Figure 6.23*. Check out the official link for the `pi-camera npm` module at `https://www.npmjs.com/package/pi-camera`:

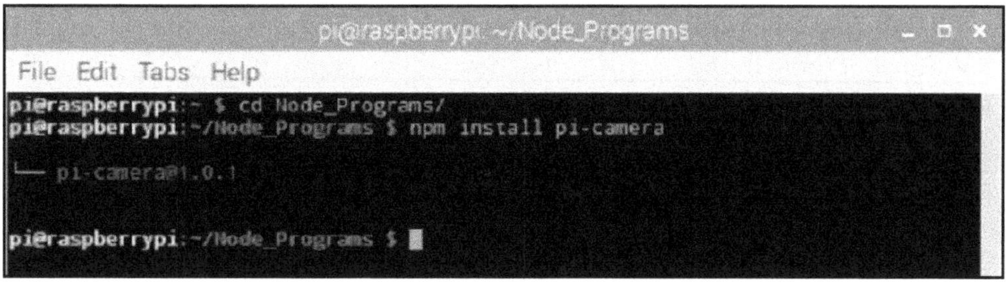

Figure 6.23

Now, create a file with the name `CameraModule.js` and include the `pi-camera` module in it:

```
const PiCamera = require('pi-camera');
```

As per the documentation of the `pi-camera` module, we need to set the configuration of the camera. We define both configurations, one for taking still pictures and the other for taking videos:

```
const myCameraPhoto = new PiCamera({
    mode: 'photo',
    output: `/home/pi/Node_Programs/photos/photo.jpg`,
    width: 640,
    height: 480
  });
const myCameraVideo = new PiCamera({
    mode: 'video',
    output: `/home/pi/Node_Programs/videos/video.h264`,
    width: 1920,
    height: 1080,
   timeout: 5000
  });
```

In both configurations, we define the following:

- A mode that defines whether the camera takes still photographs or a video. Note that the video is created in the `h246` format, which is the raw format, and can be viewed using quite a few popular video players. I use VLC media player to play video with the extension `h246`.
- The output that defines the path where the photo or video will be saved in local storage.

- The height and width that define the resolution.
- Timeout (only in the case of video) defines the length of the video that will be recorded.

We define a `cameraInUse` flag and set it to `false` by default. This flag make sure that, when the camera is busy taking pictures or recording a video, it doesn't accept any further requests until it is free; otherwise, it might cause an error while loading the camera:

```
var camerInUse = false;
```

Now, we define a function that will take a picture when called. This function takes `callback` as an argument and returns a success message when the picture is clicked successfully.

Note that we use `module.exports` to define the function, which will make this function available when `CameraModule.js` is included (imported) in other modules. Also, we will follow this practice throughout the chapter for other modules as well:

```
module.exports.takePicture = function (callback){
  if (camerInUse == false) {
    camerInUse = true;
    myCameraPhoto.snap()
    .then((result) => {
    console.log('Your picture was captured')
    callback('success')
    camerInUse = false;
  })
    .catch((error) => {
    console.log(error.toString());
    callback(error.toString());
    });
    }
  else {
    console.log('camera in use..')
    }
}
```

Before taking a picture, the code will check whether the camera is in use or not by checking whether the value of the `cameraInUse` flag is `false`; once the camera starts to take a photo, the flag is set to true so that no further requests are accepted for the camera until the photo is taken and the flag is again set to `false`.

Similarly, we define a function that will record the video when called:

```
module.exports.takeVideo = function (callback) {
  if(camerInUse == false){
    camerInUse = true;
  myCameraVideo.record()
    .then((result) => {
    console.log('recording completed...!!');
    callback('success')
    camerInUse = false;
  })
    .catch((error) => {
    console.log(error.toString());
  });
  }
  else{
    console.log('camera in use..')
  }
}
```

Email module code

The email module is used for sending the email notification whenever a trespasser enters our premises along with evidence in the form of a video or photograph as an attachment with the email.

To accomplish this task, we use the npm module nodemailer. Download this by running the npm install nodemailer command in the terminal as shown in *Figure 6.24*. Check out the official link for the nodemailer npm module at https://www.npmjs.com/package/nodemailer.

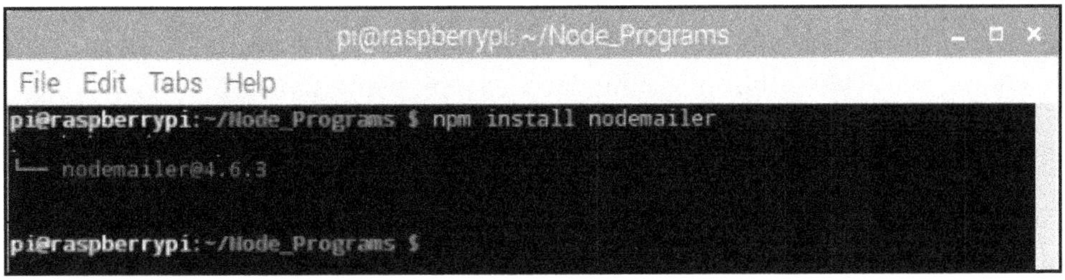

Figure 6.24

Create a file with the name `EmailModule.js` and include the `nodemailer` module in it.

```
var nodemailer = require('nodemailer');
```

Now, we set the transport configuration for the email module by providing the details of the email service provider (we use Gmail), the email ID from which the email will be sent, and its username and password:

```
var transporter = nodemailer.createTransport({
  service: 'gmail',
    auth: {
      user: 'YOUR_EMAIL_ADDRESS',
      pass: 'PASSWORD'
    }
});
```

Next, we set the email options for sending the email with the video and photo as attachment:

```
const videoMailOptions = {
  from: YOUR_EMAIL_ADDRESS',
  to: 'RECEPIENT_EMAIL_ADDRESS',
  subject: 'Intruder in your Castle...!!',
  html: '&lt;p>Some one is trying to steal your gold...!!&lt;/p>',
  attachments: [{
    filename: 'IntruderVideo.h264',
      path: '/home/pi/Node_Programs/videos/video.h264'
    }]
};
```

Here we define the following:

- `from`: This is the email address of the sender of the email
- `to`: This is the email address of the recipient of the email
- `subject`: This is the subject line of the email being sent
- `Html`: This is the content of the email
- `attachments`: This includes the following elements:
    - `filename`: Here, you can set the name of the file which is sent as an attachment
    - `path`: This is the local file storage path from where the file will be picked for attachment

Similarly, we define the email option for sending still photos as shown in the following block of code:

```
const photoMailOptions = {
  from: YOUR_EMAIL_ADDRESS',
  to: 'RECEPIENT_EMAIL_ADDRESS',
  subject: 'Intruder in your Castle...!!',
  html: '&lt;p>Someone is trying to steal your gold...!!&lt;/p>',
  attachments: [{
    filename: 'IntruderImage.jpg',
      path: '/home/pi/Node_Programs/photos/photo.jpg'
  }]
};
```

Now, we write functions that will send the email whenever triggered. We have written separate functions for both video and photo emails:

```
module.exports.sendMailVideo = function () {
  transporter.sendMail(videoMailOptions, function (err, info) {
    if(err){
      console.log(err.toString());
    }
    else{
      console.log('Video email success..!!');
    }
  });
}

module.exports.sendMailPhoto = function (){
  transporter.sendMail(photoMailOptions, function (err, info) {
    if(err){
      console.log(err.toString())
    }
    else{
      console.log('Photo email success..!!');
    }
  });
}
```

Sensor module code

Now, we write the code for sensor modules, which will govern the functioning of all the sensors and LED. To accomplish our task, we need an `npm` module called `pigpio`, which gives us access to the GPIO of Raspberry Pi. To install the `pigpio` module, run the `sudo npm install pigpio` command in the terminal as shown in *Figure 6.25*:

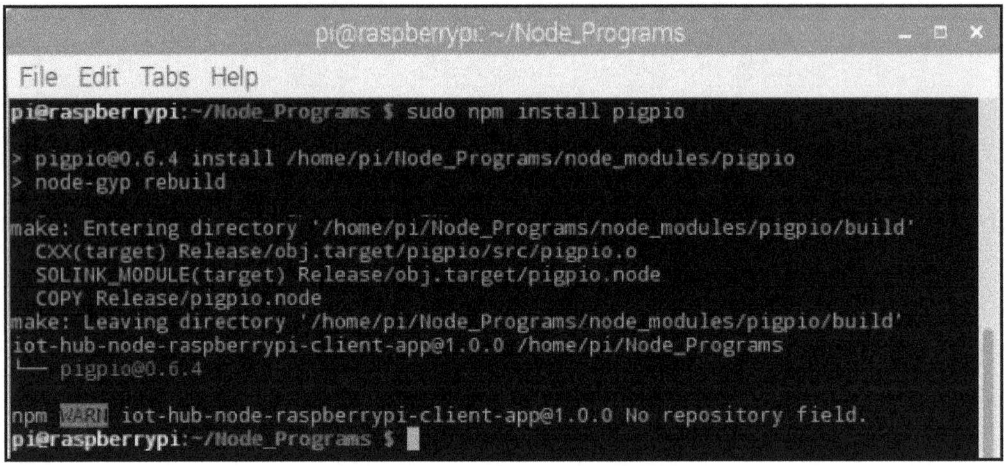

Figure 6.25

Check out the official `npm` link at `https://www.npmjs.com/package/pigpio` for more details about the `pigpio` module.

Create a file with the name `Survillance.js` and include the `pigpio` module. We also include `CameraModule.js` and `EmailModule.js`, which we developed in the previous section. This will give access to the functions of each module for taking pictures, videos, and sending emails:

```
var GPIO = require('pigpio').Gpio,
cameraModule = require('./CameraModule'),
emailModule = require('./EmailModule');
```

Make sure that files `Survillance.js`, `EmailModule.js`, and `CameraModule.js` are placed in the same directory.

As per the connection we made in the *Wiring up* section, we initialize the Raspberry Pi's pins for reading out and sending signals to sensors and LEDs:

```
var PIR_out= new GPIO(19,{mode: GPIO.INPUT,alert: true}),
red_LED= new GPIO(17,{mode: GPIO.OUTPUT}),
buzzer= new GPIO(26,{mode: GPIO.OUTPUT}),
IR_out= new GPIO(5,{mode: GPIO.INPUT,alert: true}),
trigger = new GPIO(16, {mode: GPIO.OUTPUT}),
echo = new GPIO(21, {mode: GPIO.INPUT, alert: true});
```

The PIR sensor's output (PIR_out) is connected to GPIO 19, so we declared GPIO 19 as the input and set the alert event flag to true. The alert event indicates that whenever the value at the GPIO changes from low (0) to high (1) or vice versa, then an alert event will be raised. We can listen to the alert event and take action accordingly.

The positive terminal of LED (red_LED) is connected to GPIO 17. The LED will work as an indicator; whenever a trespasser is detected, the LED will glow. GPIO 17 is set as the OUTPUT pin.

The buzzer is connected to the Pi with one of its terminals connected to GPIO 26 and the other connected to the ground. The buzzer is used to raise an alarm when an intruder is detected, so we make GPIO 26 as OUTPUT.

The infrared sensor's output (IR_out) is connected to GPIO 5, which is declared as the INPUT pin, and the alert event flag is set to true as we did for the PIR sensor.

The trigger terminal of the ultrasonic sensor is used to generate high frequency ultrasonic waves. The trigger pin is connected to GPIO 16, so we declared it as the OUTPUT pin.

The echo pin of the ultrasonic sensor is connected to GPIO 21. The echo pin is used to get the output of the ultrasonic sensor, so it is declared as INPUT and the alert event flag is set to true.

Make sure you initialize the LED to low (0) level:

```
red_LED.digitalWrite(0);
```

Let's first write the code block to read the data of the PIR sensor:

```
PIR_out.on('alert', function(level, tick){
  if(level==1) {
  cameraModule.takePicture(function (callback) {
  var result = callback;
  if (result == 'success') {
      emailModule.sendMailPhoto()
```

```
      }
    })
    console.log('PIR : Intruder Alert..!!')
    red_LED.digitalWrite(level);
    buzzer.digitalWrite(level);
  }
  else {
    red_LED.digitalWrite(level);
    buzzer.digitalWrite(level);
  }
})
```

Here, we listen to the `alert` event for the PIR sensor. As soon as the PIR sensor detects any trespasser in the house, the output goes high from the initial low state, which causes an `alert` event to fire. The `alert` function returns a callback with two parameters: one is `level` and the other one is `tick`. The `level` indicates the state of the GPIO at that moment and `tick` is the timestamp at which the change in state is observed at the GPIO. So we check the alert event and if the level is high (1), then we immediately take a photo of the trespasser by calling the `takePicture` function of the camera module; then, we raise the alarm by setting the output of the buzzer and LED indicator to high. Once we receive the `success` as callback from the camera module's `takePicture` function, we call the `sendMailPhoto` function of the email module, which will send the alert email along with the photo of the trespasser to the owner of the house.

Now, we write the code for the IR sensor, which is very much similar to the PIR sensor code:

```
IR_out.on('alert', function(level, tick){
  if(level==1){
    cameraModule.takeVideo(function (callback) {
      var result = callback;
      if(result == 'success'){
        emailModule.sendMailVideo() ;
      }
    })
    console.log('IR : Intruder Alert..!!'
    red_LED.digitalWrite(level);
    buzzer.digitalWrite(level);
  }
  else {
    red_LED.digitalWrite(level);
    buzzer.digitalWrite(level);
  }
})
```

An IR sensor works in the exact same way as the PIR sensor. The only difference is that we take a video recording instead of taking a still photo.

Lastly, we write the code block for an ultrasonic sensor module:

```
  trigger.digitalWrite(0);
var MICROSECDONDS_PER_CM = 1000000/33000;
// Trigger a distance measurement once per second
  setInterval(function () {
  trigger.trigger(10, 1); // Set trigger high for 10 microseconds
  }, 5000);
//The number of microseconds it takes sound to travel 1cm at 20 degrees
celcius
var startTick;
  echo.on('alert', function (level, tick) {
    var endTick,
    diff;
    if (level == 1) {
      startTick = tick;
    }
    else {
      endTick = tick;
      diff = (endTick >> 0) - (startTick >> 0); //Unsigned 32-bit
arithmetic
      var actualDist = (diff / 2 / MICROSECDONDS_PER_CM) ;
        if (actualDist &lt;10){
      console.log('Ultrasonic : Intruder Detected...!!')
      red_LED.digitalWrite(1);
      buzzer.digitalWrite(level);
      cameraModule.takePicture(function (callback) {
        var result = callback;
        if (result == 'success'){
          emailModule.sendMailPhoto() }
        })
      }
      else {
        red_LED.digitalWrite(0);
        buzzer.digitalWrite(0);
      }
    }
});
```

Making use of the trigger function of the `pigpio` module, we send a high pulse on the trigger pin of the ultrasonic sensor for 10 microseconds, which causes the sensor transmitter to emit a burst 8 high-frequency pulse, which makes the output at the echo pin high.

The output of the ultrasonic sensor is taken from the Echo pin on which we are listening for the `alert` event. As soon as the ultrasonic wave is transmitted, the state of the Echo pin changes to high and the `alert` event is fired, which returns a callback with two parameters. The first is the `level`, which is used to check whether the state of echo is high (1) or low (0) and the other is `tick`, which is used to check the timestamp when the state changed. The state of the echo is changed from low to high and we save this timestamp as `startTick`. When the waves get reflected from obstruction and fall on the receiver, the state of the Echo pin is changed from high to low; we save this timestamp as `endTick`. Now, to get the distance of the obstruction from the sensor, we need to get the time the ultrasonic waves took to travel, to and from the sensor to obstruction and back to the sensor; we need to subtract `startTick` from `endTick`. The `tick` is actually the number of microseconds since the system boot. Its value is an unsigned 32-bit quantity. So, to get the correct value after subtraction, we use the right shift operator.

Once we have the travel time, we then calculate the distance using the formula knowing the wave speed (330 m/s). This means that, in 1 second, ultrasonic waves travel 330 meters (in 1,000,000 micro seconds the waves travel 33,000 cm).

Once we have the distance, we then check whether the distance is less than 10 cm. If it is, we raise an alert by lighting the LED, beeping the Buzzer, taking a picture, and finally sending the alert through email.

We have completed the code part. Now, let's execute the code by running the command in the terminal:

```
sudo node Survillance.js
```

We have written a few statements to log the data on the console to understand the execution of this code block. The output for the PIR sensor is shown in the console (as shown in *Figure 6.26*):

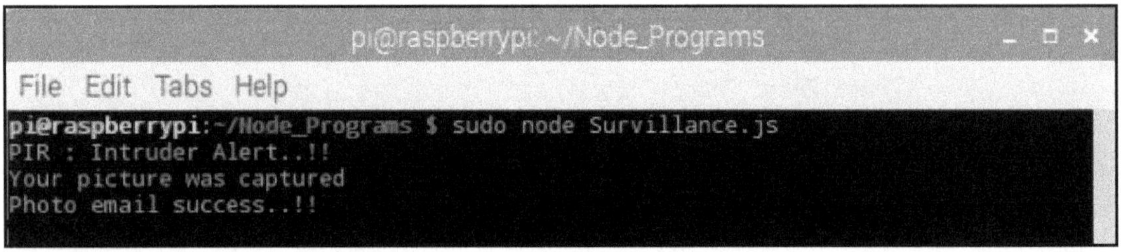

Figure 6.26

The output of the IR sensor is shown in *Figure 6.27*:

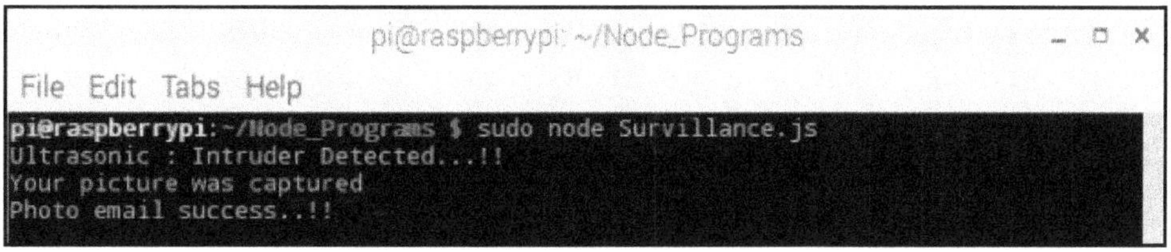

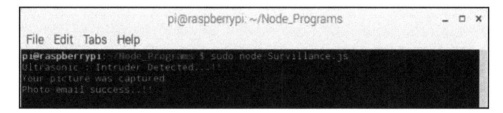

Figure 6.27

The output of the ultrasonic sensor is shown in *Figure 6.28*:

Figure 6.28

Figure 6.29 shows a snapshot of the email notification received as an alert:

Figure 6.29

Summary

During our journey through this chapter, we discussed IR sensors, PIR sensors, and ultrasonic sensors in detail. We have also learned how to use Raspberry Pi camera module and how to send email notification programmatically; finally we stitched together all the components to build a security surveillance system. Now, we can go out without worrying about the security of our home in our absence.

In Chapter 7, *Image Recognition*, we will learn about face recognition techniques and build a face recognition system using Raspberry Pi.

7
Image Recognition

In this chapter, we will understand what image recognition is, how image recognition works, and how we train a machine to recognize images. Then, we will learn about all the resources that are required to perform image recognition tasks. The following are the resources that we will cover in this chapter:

- Raspberry Pi
- Raspberry Pi camera module to capture real-time images
- IR sensor
- Amazon Web Services
- Amazon's IAM service
- Amazon's command-line interface
- Amazon's S3 storage service to store the captured images
- Amazon's Rekognition web services, which we will use to perform image recognition

Understanding image recognition

Image recognition is the ability of a machine or computer to see and identify places, logos, people, objects, buildings, and other variables in an image, where an image can be any graphic, still photo, and/or video. Image recognition not only identifies the content in the images, but performs a large number of machine-based visual tasks, such as labeling images with informational tags, searching the content in an image, such as identifying a cat in an image that has multiple animals in it and guiding autonomous robots and self-driving vehicles.

Human and animal brains recognize images and objects with ease, but it is extremely difficult for computers to perform the same task. Image recognition requires deep machine learning techniques. Image recognition tasks are best performed on convolution neural network-based processors. Image recognition algorithms perform tasks by use of comparative 3D models, comparing images taken from different angles using edge-detection techniques. These algorithms need to be trained with millions of already labeled pictures with guided computer learning.

Deep learning

Let's understand what deep learning is. Deep learning is a part of machine learning that deals with emulating the learning approach of human beings. Traditional machine learning algorithms are linear in nature, whereas deep learning algorithms are nonlinear and stacked in a hierarchy of increasing complexity and abstraction, for example, when the parents of a toddler teach him what a cat looks like by pointing at it, and when he points to an object the next time and tags it as a cat, then the parents confirm by saying *"Yes, it is a cat"* or if the toddler identifies it wrongly, then the parents say *"No, it is not a cat."* In this way, a toddler learns to identify a cat and makes himself aware of all the features of a cat over a period of time. In this process, what a toddler does is unconsciously build a stack of information in their mind about a cat, where each layer of this information in the stack is created using the information from the previous layer. Every next layer of information becomes more complex and weighted than the previous one. A deep learning algorithm applies the same technique to learn and identify the content of images that are fed to it.

In traditional machine learning, the learning is supervised, where the programmer has to specifically define all the features of an object that the algorithm should look for and identify in an image that is fed to it as input. The programmer has to define the feature of a cat (object) and tag the cat in the training dataset. This process is called feature extraction, which is very time consuming. Also, the accuracy of the result depends on how efficiently the features are defined and the object is tagged in the input dataset.

The advantage of deep machine learning (or simply deep learning) over traditional machine learning is that the programmer is not required to do the feature extraction task by themselves. Here, the software program creates the feature list by itself; hence, deep learning is called unsupervised learning, which is not only fast but more accurate than supervised learning.

To implement deep learning, we need to provide the training dataset, which contains the images tagged as cat or no cat. Then, the program uses the input images to extract the features of a cat and build a model around it to predict a cat in a new dataset, which is untagged. This model is called the predictive model. The deep learning algorithm looks for patterns in pixels from digital image data and with each iteration, the predictive model becomes more complex and accurate. Unlike a toddler, who takes a long time to accurately identify a cat every time, the deep learning algorithm can do it in minutes. So, to achieve an acceptable level of accuracy, deep learning algorithms need huge volumes of data and processing power.

Since deeplearning techniques depict the human brain, they are sometimes called neural networks. There are different types of neural networks such as recurrent neural networks, convolutional neural networks, artificial neural networks, and feed forward neural networks. Each one of them has its own implementation and use cases.

Deep learning is mostly used in image recognition, natural language processing, and speech recognition tools.

The limitation of deep learning is that it knows only what has been taught to it. This means that if it is trained to identify a cat, then it cannot identify a dog by itself. And to identify the cat accurately, it needs huge volumes of pretagged training data, which is not an easy task. Additionally, there are issues of bias in the results because if the training dataset contains only a black cat, then it might not identify a white cat, which is a biased decision against white cats.

How image recognition works

Image recognition works on the principal of image classification, where classification is pattern matching within the data. Images are data in the form of two-dimensional matrices.

There are four major steps in the image recognition process. The first is gathering data, the second is organizing data, the third is building a predictive model, and the last one is recognizing image.

Gathering data

When the human eye sees any image, it perceives it as signals, which then fall on the visual cortex of the brain through the eyes. The visual cortex then processes these signals, which results in the experience of the scene. These scenes are then compared with the concepts and objects stored in one's memory and interpreted accordingly. Similarly, when an image in digital form is fed to the computer, it perceives the image as either a raster or vector image.

Raster images (graphics) are bitmaps. A bitmap is a grid of individual pixels that together make up an image. Each pixel in a bitmap is coded with specific shades of a color. Raster graphics are used for nonlinear art images such as digital photographs and scanned images.

Vector images (graphics) are based on mathematical formulas that define geometric properties of images such as circles, polygons, lines, curves, and rectangles. Vector graphics are used to represent structured images such as line art and images with flat and uniform colors.

Let's see an example of an image (refer to *Figure 7.1*) and its representation in vector form (refer to *Figure 7.2*), and raster form (refer to *Figure 7.3*):

Figure 7.1 (original image)

Raster image: This is made up of pixels:

Figure 7.2

Vector image: This is made up of geometric figures, circles:

Figure 7.3

Organizing data

Organizing data involves image classification and feature extraction. In an image, there are some extra sets of features, which might not be of any significance to us. These extra features may be part of the background in an image or may be noise generated while converting the image into digital format. So, an image is made up of informative and important patterns combined with insignificant patterns.

In the image classification process, we extract the important and required features and leave out the rest. important features, we suppress and normalize the insignificant features and highlight the important features in an image. To extract these features, we use edge detection. Edge detection is a technique to find out the boundaries of an object in an image by detecting discontinuities in brightness. The image pixels of the object and the rest of the image background differ greatly in intensity and color, which forms the edge.

There are some well-known feature extraction techniques, namely HAAR-like features, Histogram of Oriented Gradients (HOG), Scale Invariant Feature Transform (SIFT), and Speed Up Robust Feature (SURF).

Building a predictive model

In the previous step, we converted the image into a feature vector and now we will see how the classification algorithm takes this feature vector as input and identifies the object accurately. To make sure that our algorithm works with high accuracy, we need to train it with large volumes of data that contains the object to be identified. If the object to be identified is a cat, for example, then we will feed the algorithm training data of cat and non-cat images.

The principal of machine learning algorithm is to treat the feature vector as points in higher dimensional space. Then, it finds out the planes and surfaces that separate higher dimensional space, which enables it to separate the object to be identified from the rest of the image.

To build a predictive model around this, we need a neural network system. The neural network system consists of large number of a interconnected nodes, and each node is a combination of hardware and software. The neural network uses one of the many classification algorithms available, such as bag-of-words, **Support Vector Machine** (**SVM**), face landmark estimation, **K-Nearest Neighbors** (**KNN**), and logistic regression.

Recognizing an image

This is the last and easiest step in the image recognition task. We provide the input data that contains both the training dataset and the test dataset. The training dataset has images tagged as cat and not cat. Once the model is trained, the test data, which contains images without tags, is processed and it identifies the closest resemblance to a cat from it.

There are a few major challenges in building an image recognition system and the most important one is the hardware issue. In the case of high definition images, the training set of few thousand images amounts to a few billion pixel values to be computed. The computation is not linear, but complex derivatives, which require a lot of computing power. To overcome these challenges, the following points should be taken care of:

- Use image compression tools that reduce the size of images without compromising on image quality
- Use grayscale and gradient versions of colored images
- Use a **Graphical Processor Unit** (**GPU**), which provides good computation power

Since we have understood the basics of how image recognition works, let's now perform the image recognition task. As mentioned in the introduction, we will use Amazon's S3, IAM, and Rekognition web services along with Raspberry Pi, its camera module, and an IR sensor.

Let's get into the details of each component of our project.

Amazon Web Services

Amazon Web Services (**AWS**) is an infrastructure service provided by Amazon. It provides cloud computing services. Their services are available in a pay-as-you-go model, which means you just have to pay for what you use.

AWS has dozens of actual physical data centers spread across **Availability Zones** (**AZs**) in multiple regions across the world. An *AZ* represents a single location that contains multiple data centers and a *Region* is an area that contains multiple AZs in close proximity to each other.

All the services that are provided can be accessed from an AWS account from anywhere in the world. For example, we can start any virtual machine with the operating system of our choice in just a few minutes. There are database services for both SQL (such as MySQL and PostgreSQL) and NoSQL (such as Dynamo DB), storage services such as S3, which can store any kind of data without any limit, AI, and machine learning services such as Rekognition. All these services are highly scalable, reliable, and available with almost zero downtime.

To know more about AWS and its services, you can visit https://aws.amazon.com/.

In our project, we will use S3, IAM, CLI, and Rekognition services. Let's learn about each service in detail.

AWS S3

Amazon S3 stands for a simple storage service, and it provides a storage facility for the internet. S3 allows to store and retrieve any amount of data from anywhere. There are multiple ways of storing and retrieving data, such as through the **Command Line Interface (CLI)**, through the API/SDK, and through the AWS management console.

S3 stores data in the form of objects inside buckets. The object inside the bucket has a file and its metadata, which has information about the file. To store an object in S3, first we need to create a bucket, then upload the object (file), and after uploading we can set the access permission for that particular object inside the bucket. Apart from access, we can also set the geographical region (out of the available ones) in which the bucket should be placed. Figure 7.4 shows a general flow of task performed in S3:

Figure 7.4

Let's perform all the steps one by one to experience how S3 works:

1. Once you create and log in to the AWS account using the AWS management console, click on **Services** in the top left. This will show all the available services, and from the available services, select S3 as shown in *Figure 7.5*:

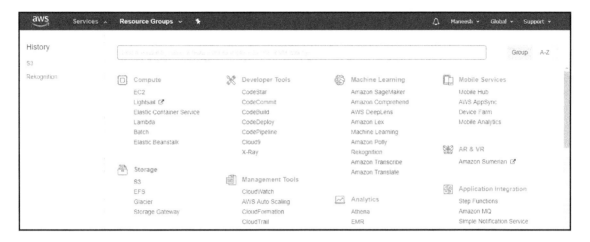

Figure 7.5

2. Under S3, there are options to create, delete, and empty buckets. Since we do not have any buckets available, we will create a new one by selecting the **Create a new bucket** option, as shown in *Figure 7.6*:

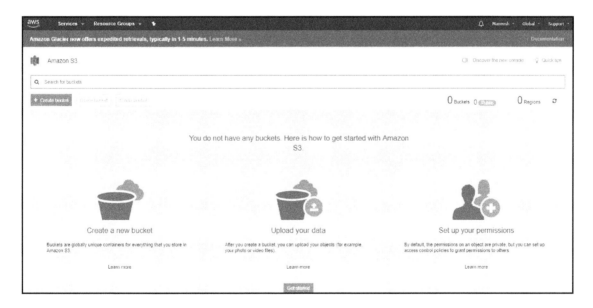

Figure 7.6

3. A pop-up window will appear in which we need to provide details such as **Bucket name** and **Region** to create the bucket, as shown in *Figure 7.7*:

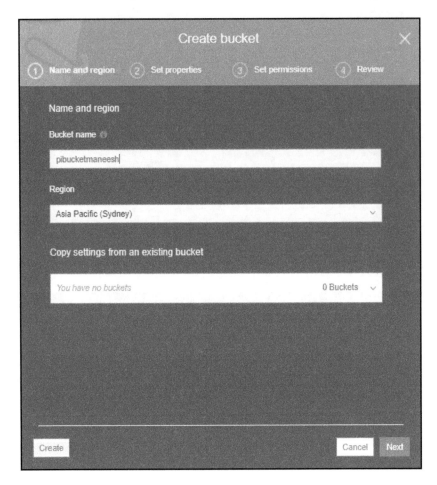

Figure 7.7

4. Click on **Next** for the next three steps by setting properties, setting permission, and finally saving the configuration and creating a bucket. After successful bucket creation, it will appear in S3 as shown in *Figure 7.8*:

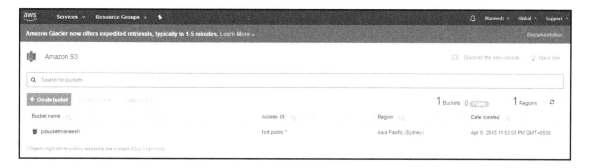

Figure 7.8

AWS Rekognition

Rekognition is one of the AI/machine learning services provided by AWS. This is basically a computer vision-based service, which allow us to do analysis of videos and images without having to write all the algorithms by ourselves. We just need to provide a video or image as input to the Rekognition service and it will identify objects, texts, people, scenes, and activities. It also provides an accurate facial analysis and recognition service.

AWS Rekognition is based on deep learning technology, which we have already discussed in an earlier section of this chapter.

It provides an easy-to-use API/SDK to implement solutions. Rekognition takes data from the S3 storage service to perform the analysis.

The common use cases for which Rekognition is used are as follows:

- **Searchable image and video libraries**: This allows you to search huge volumes of videos and images for any particular object, for example, search for a cat in the entire video and image library.
- **Face-based user authentication**: This helps you compare the user's live image with the reference image and based on the result, provide or restrict access.
- **Sentiment and demographic analysis:** This allows you to detect the face and analyze the mood of a person, such as sad, happy, or angry. It also determines the gender of the person.

- **Facial recognition:** This allows you to search the images, stored videos, and live streaming videos for faces that match the known faces stored in a container called a *collection*. A collection is an index of reference faces that are stored and managed in the cloud. The two main steps in this task are as follows:
  - Index the faces
  - Search the faces

- **Unsafe content detection:** This helps you to analyze the images and videos for unsafe content that can be removed or blocked from anywhere.

There are many other applications, which you can check on the AWS website later. For our use case image/ facial recognition, we will focus on select features of Rekognition.

As mentioned earlier, Rekognition can store information on detected faces in containers called collections. Then, this stored information is used to compare to the information from target images, which are fed to the service.

The first step in this task is `IndexFaces`. When a reference image is given to the system, we perform the `IndexFaces` task, which will analyze the image data, identify the faces in it, and store all the metadata for all the faces in that image in a collection. To store the information, we need to create a collection first, which we will do while implementing the task.

The next step is to upload the input image to the S3 bucket because Rekognition takes the input data from S3 storage.

Once the input image is uploaded, we will call the `SearchFacesByImage` method. This method first detects the faces in the input image and then extracts feature information for each face, and finally compares them with the existing face information data of the reference image present in the collection. If the face match is successful, it gives the response as a confidence level in %, which means how much confidence the system has in claiming that these two faces are similar. This is how we will develop our solution.

Before we start the implementation of the project, we first need to create a user in the AWS account that will have access to S3 and the Rekognition service. This is required because using the root user to provide access to the service is not the best practice. If someone gets hold of the access key and password of our root user, then the AWS account can be hacked. So to avoid this situation, we create an **Identity and Access Management** (**IAM**) user, which will have access to only S3 and Rekognition.

Identity and access management

Let's create an IAM user in AWS using the management console:

1. Log in to the AWS account in the top left and click on services, and then click on **IAM** under **Security, Identity & Compliance**, as shown in *Figure 7.9*:

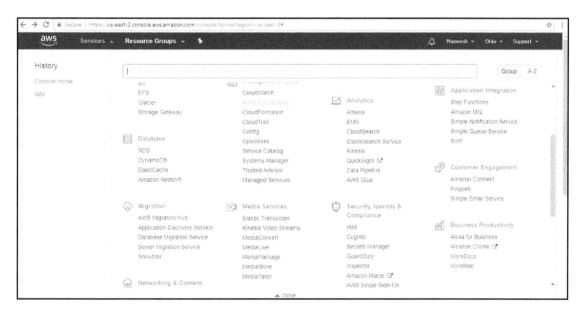

Figure 7.9

2. Under IAM, click on users as shown in *Figure 7.10*:

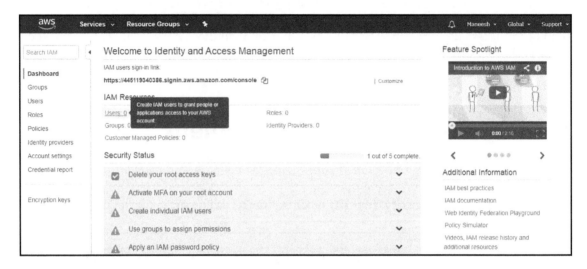

Figure 7.10

3. In the next tab, click on **Add users** as shown in *Figure 7.11*:

Figure 7.11

4. In the next tab, provide a **User name**. For access type, check the **programmatic access** checkbox and click on **Next Permissions,** as shown in *Figure 7.12*:

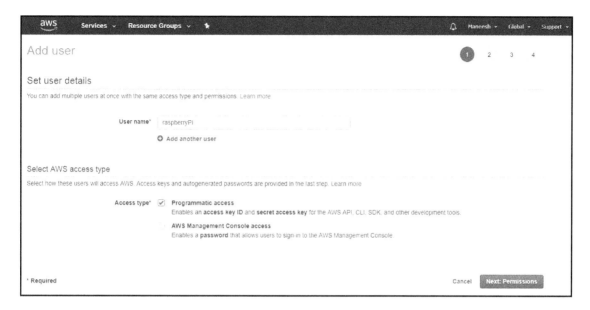

Figure 7.12

5. In the next tab, we need to provide permissions for this user to access S3 and Rekognition, as shown in *Figure 7.13* and *Figure 7.14*, respectively:

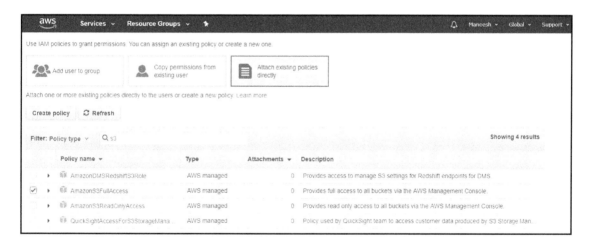

Figure 7.13

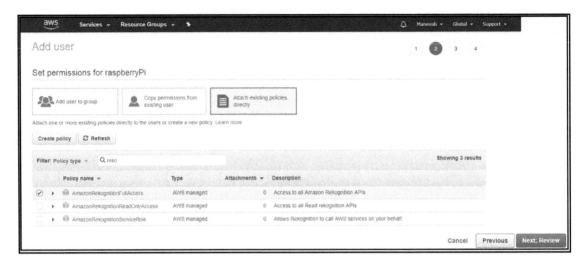

Figure 7.14

6. In the next step, click on **See the preview** for both S3 and Rekognition and click on **Create user**. Once a user with a defined set of permissions is created successfully, it will provide the credentials in a `.csv` file, which can be downloaded as shown in *Figure 7.15*:

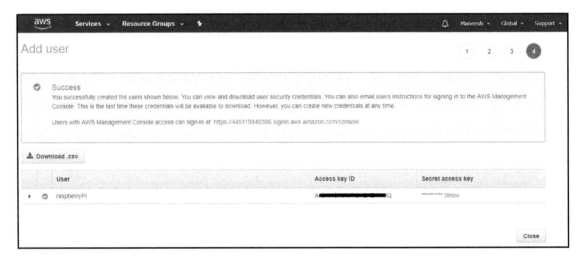

Figure 7.15

Do not forget to download the credential file because after closing the tab, the credentials cannot be retrieved for that user again.

Command line interface

Command Line Interface (CLI) is a tool used to perform all AWS operations from the command window. Here, we will use this tool to create a collection for the Rekognition service.

The system used to develop this is Windows, so we will use the CLI installer provided by AWS for this. For your OS-specific installation method, refer to the following URL:
`https://docs.aws.amazon.com/cli/latest/userguide/installing.html`
Download the `.msi` installed from the following URL:
`https://docs.aws.amazon.com/cli/latest/userguide/awscli-install-windows.html`

1. Download and run the installer, then follow the onscreen steps to complete the installation. After a successful download, open Command Prompt and execute the `aws --version` command to check the version of AWS CLI, as shown in *Figure 7.19*:

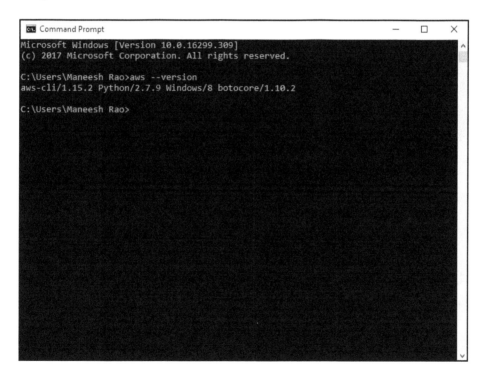

Figure 7.19

2. Before we use CLI to perform any operation, we need to configure it with the username, password, and region. Run the `aws configure` command in Command Prompt and provide the information asked for, as shown in *Figure 7.20*:

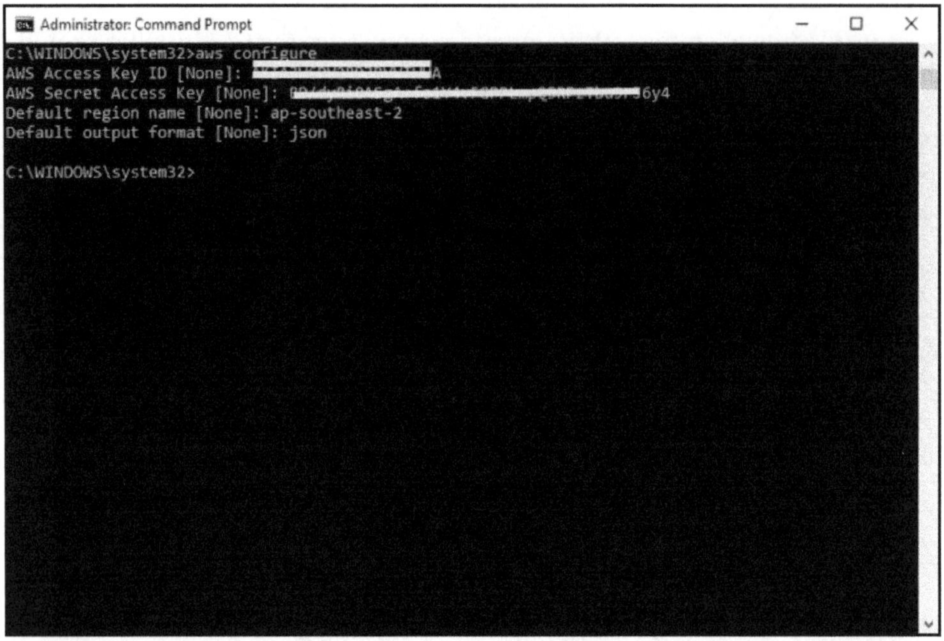

Figure 7.20

As we have already learned to use Raspberry Pi, its camera module, and an IR sensor in the previous chapter, we will not cover them again here.

Implementation

Using all the building blocks discussed until now, we will build an image recognition-based building access management system. This system has three main components.

The first is creating the collection, which will store the feature information of all the images.

The second is where the image of a new person is uploaded for the first time in the face collection. This task is executed automatically when the person stands in front of the IR sensor (interfaced with Raspberry Pi). The sensor detects their presence and triggers the camera to capture the image of their face. Then, the image is uploaded in S3 and the `IndexFaces` operation is performed, which extracts the feature information from the face and stores it in a collection.

In the third component, when a person stands near the entrance, an IR sensor detects their presence and triggers the camera to capture the image of the standing person. Then, the captured picture is compared with the reference images already stored in the system, using the `SearchFacesByImage` method. It compares the face by extracting the features of the face in the image and if the two faces match, it allows the person to enter the building (glow LED), and if not, it raises an alert.

Figure 7.21 shows the architecture of our implementation:

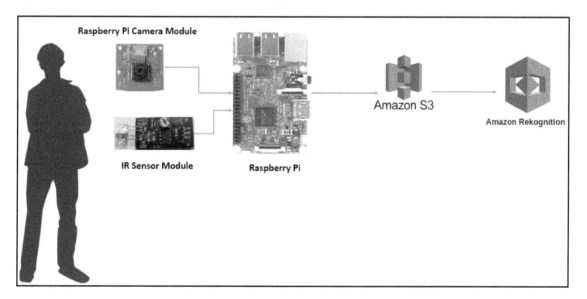

Figure 7.21

Let's begin with the implementation step by step.

Create collection

The collection will store information about all the reference faces. With these reference faces, we will compare the input faces. To create a collection, we will use the CLI tool. Open Command Prompt and run the following command, shown in *Figure 7.22*. We need to provide a collection ID as a parameter while executing the command:

```
aws rekognition create-collection –collection-id "piCollection"
```

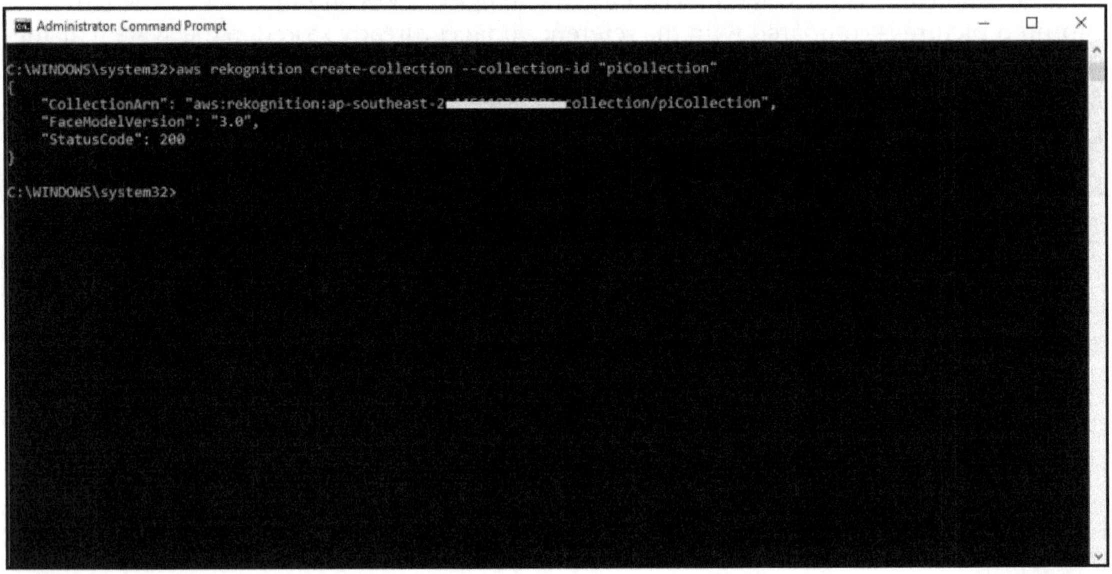

Figure 7.22

In response to the create-collection command, we receive a JSON object, which contains CollecetionARn,a version of the Rekognition service, and status code.

Upload reference image

This particular task consists of multiple smaller tasks. Here, we take a picture of a person for the first time and upload it to S3. Then, we run the IndexFaces function on it, which extracts the features of the face in the image and stores it in the collection created in the previous step.

We have implemented this in such a manner that when a person stands in front of the camera, the IR sensor detects their presence and triggers the camera to capture the image. The captured image is then uploaded to S3, on which the `IndexFaces` operation is performed. After successful execution, an LED will light up. Refer to *Figure 7.23* to understand the flow of this part:

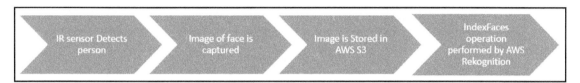

Figure 7.23

The actual image upload part will look similar to what is shown in *Figure 7.24*:

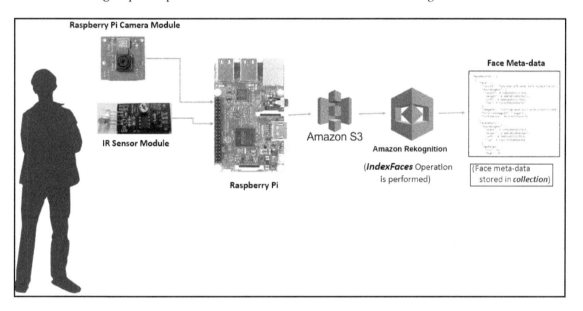

Figure 7.24

Face comparison

In this part, when a person tries to enter the building through the gate, the IR sensor detects the presence and captures the image of the person. Then, this image is stored in the S3 bucket and from there it is passed to Rekognition, which then uses the `SearchFacesByImage` method to compare the face with the existing data present in the collection. If the face matches the existing data, it means that the person is authentic and is then allowed to enter. Refer to *Figure 7.25*, which shows the flow of information for face comparison:

Figure 7.25

The actual face comparison part will look similar to what is shown in *Figure 7.26*:

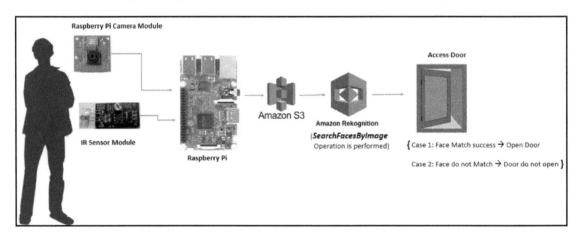

Figure 7.26

Wiring up

Now, we will wire the hardware component to complete our circuit. Note that in actual scenario of building access management there will be two separate systems, one for adding people to the authentic list where a picture of that person is taken for the first time and stored for matching purposes in future. In the other systems when a person tries to enter the building, the system will capture the image in real time and then do a comparison with a collection of authentic faces (this collection is created while adding people to the Authentic list for the first time). If the faces match successfully, that means the person is authentic and allowed to enter; otherwise they are not allowed to enter.

So, these two system will have separate hardware and circuits, but in our case, we will use the same hardware and circuits to demonstrate the working of the whole concept.

Interfacing IR sensor

Refer to *Figure 7.26* for connection details:

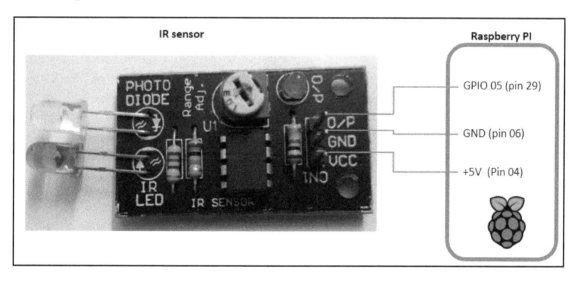

Figure 7.26

Interfacing LEDs

Since we choose not to use the actual door and lock system, we will use LEDs to indicate door open, door close, and for other indication purposes. Refer to *Figure 7.27* for connection details:

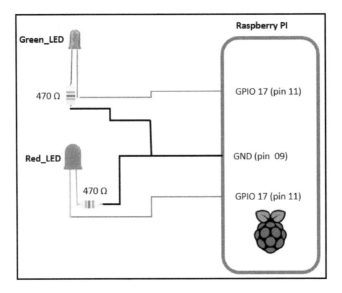

Figure 7.27

Interfacing the Pi camera module

This camera module can be easily interfaced to a CSI camera port that is dedicated to Raspberry Pi. This camera has a ribbon cable that attaches the camera to Pi. Check out the official video at `https://www.raspberrypi.org/documentation/usage/camera/README.md` by the Raspberry Pi Foundation to install the camera on Pi correctly.

The code

Let's write the code to bring the building access management System to life using AWS S3 and Rekognition.

The setup requires Node.js to be installed on Raspberry Pi, which we have already done quite a few times in the previous chapter. So, we'll not repeat that here and straight away start writing the code.

Index face module code

This code will extract the feature information of faces stored in the S3 bucket and store them in the `piCollection` that we created earlier using the AWS CLI tool.

Create a file with the name `indexFaces.js` and include the `npm` modules `aws-sdk` and `fs` in it. Make sure these modules are installed or run `npm install` command in the terminal to do the installation, as shown in *Figure 7.28* and *Figure 7.29*:

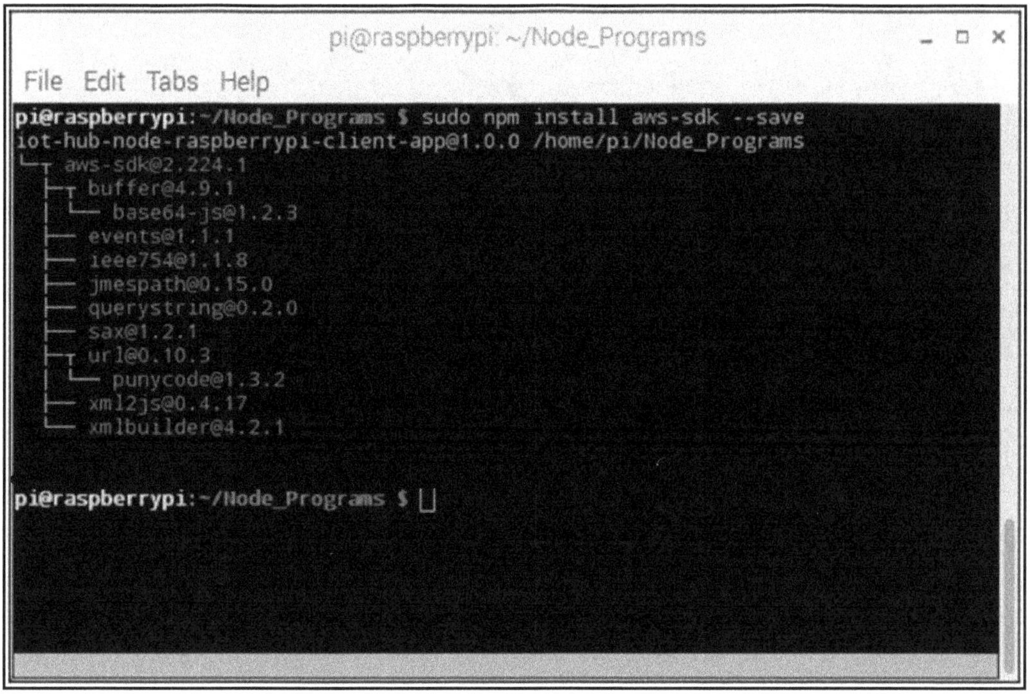

Figure 7.28

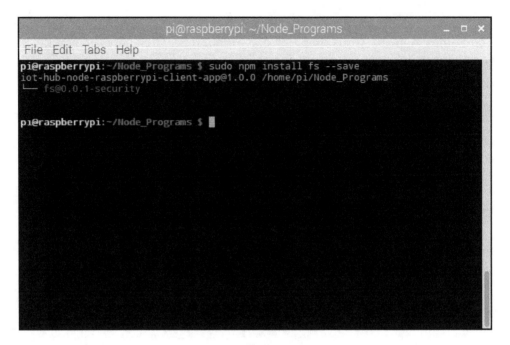

Figure 7.29

In the `indexFaces.js` file, add both modules using `require`:

```
var AWS = require('aws-sdk'),
fs = require('fs');
```

Now, we will add the access key and region configuration, which allows access to AWS services for a particular user in a particular region. Also, declare a variable to access all the methods of Rekognition:

```
AWS.config.update({

  accessKeyId: 'YOUR_ACCESS_KEY_ID',

  secretAccessKey: 'YOUR_SECRET_ACCESS_KEY'

});

AWS.config.update({region:'ap-southeast-2'});

  var rekognition = new AWS.Rekognition();
```

Next, we create a method with the name `IndexFacesMethod`, which will perform the `IndexFaces` operation. In this method, we provide the S3 bucket name, the name of the image inside the bucket, and the collection ID created in the Rekognition service as an input parameter. As an output, the `IndexFaces` method returns the metadata of the image, which contains a list of all the features extracted from faces in that image:

```
module.exports.IndexFacesMethod = function (callback) {

var params = {

  CollectionId: 'piCollection',

  Image: {

    S3Object: {

            Bucket: Name_of_S3_Bucket,

            Name: 'Name_of_Image_stored_in_S3_bucket.jpg'

        }

  },

  DetectionAttributes: [ "ALL"],

  ExternalImageId: 'ID123'

};

rekognition.indexFaces(params, function(err, data) {

  if (err) {

          console.log(err, err.stack);

          }

  else {
          console.log(JSON.stringify(data));

          callback('success')

          }
});

}
```

The `IndexFacesMethod` method is exported using `module.export`, which will become accessible from other modules when the `IndexFaces.js` module is included.

Read the details about using the `IndexFacesMethod` method at `https://docs.aws.amazon.com/AWSJavaScriptSDK/latest/AWS/Rekognition.html`.

Search face by image module code

This module takes an image from the S3 bucket as input and performs a search and comparison operation with the data stored in the collection. If a similar face is found, it will provide the output with the percentage of similarity between the input and a similar image found in the collection.

Create a file with the name `searchFacesByImage.js` and include the following code:

```javascript
var AWS = require('aws-sdk'),
        fs = require('fs');

AWS.config.update({

  accessKeyId: 'YOUR_ACCESS_KEY_ID',

  secretAccessKey: 'YOUR_SECRET_ACCESS_KEY'

});

AWS.config.update({region:'ap-southeast-2'});

  var rekognition = new AWS.Rekognition();

module.exports.searchFaceMethod = function (callback) {

var params = {

  CollectionId: 'piCollection',

  Image: {

    S3Object: {

      Bucket: 'pibucketmaneesh',

      Name: 'TargetImageS3.jpg'

    }
```

```
        },

        FaceMatchThreshold: 90.0,

        MaxFaces: 1

    };

    rekognition.searchFacesByImage(params, function(err, data) {

        if (err) {

                console.log(err, err.stack);

                }

        else {

         console.log(JSON.stringify(data));

         callback('success')

            }

        });

    }
```

Read details about using the `SearchFacesByImage` method at the following URL: `https:/
/docs.aws.amazon.com/AWSJavaScriptSDK/latest/AWS/Rekognition.html`.

S3 bucket module code

In this module, we will take the image stored in the local storage of Raspberry Pi and
upload it to the S3 bucket. On successful execution, it then calls the `IndexFaces` or
`SearchFacesByImage` function of the `IndexFaces.js` and `SearchFacesByImage.js`
modules respectively, based on which task needs to be performed. The image is taken using
a camera and camera module code, which we will cover in the next section.

Create a file with the name `S3put.js` and add the following code lines, which will include the required modules and set the configurations right:

```
var AWS = require('aws-sdk')

        fs = require('fs');

        indexfaces = require('./indexFaces'),

        searchFaces = require('./searchFacesByImage');

  AWS.config.update({

        accessKeyId: 'YOUR_ACCESS_KEY_ID',

 secretAccessKey: 'YOUR_SECRET_ACCESS_KEY'

});

AWS.config.region = 'ap-southeast-2';

var bucket = 'pibucketmaneesh';

var inputFilePathReferenceImage =
              'Path of Reference Image stored on raspberry pi for
IndexFaces operation ';

var inputFilePathTargetImage =
      'Path of input Image stored on raspberry pi for SeacrchFacesByImage
operation ';

var s3 = new AWS.S3();
```

Now, write a method that will upload the reference image to the S3 bucket and then call `IndexFacesMethod` of the `IndexFaces.js` module, which will extract the features of the face in the image and store them in the collection:

```
module.exports.uploadReferenceImageToS3 = function (callback) {

fs.readFile(inputFilePathReferenceImage, function (err, data) {

if (err) {console.log( err); }

    var base64data = new Buffer(data, 'binary');

    var params = {Bucket: bucket,
```

```
              Key: "OrigReferenceS3.jpg",

          Body: base64data};

          s3.putObject(params,function (err, data) {

if(err){console.log(err.toString())
}
else{

                  console.log(data);

                  console.log('Successfully uploaded Image.');

                  indexfaces.IndexFacesMethod(callback)

                  }

   });

      });

}
```

Now, write a method that will upload the input image to the S3 bucket and then call the searchFaceMethod method of the serachFaceByImage.js module, which will compare the features of the face in the input image with the ones stored in the collection:

```
module.exports.uploadTarget_to_S3 = function (callback) {
fs.readFile(inputFilePathTargetImage, function (err, data) {

        if (err) { throw err; }

     var base64data = new Buffer(data, 'binary');

       var params = {

              Bucket: bucket,

              Key: "TargetImageS3.jpg",

              Body: base64data

          };

   s3.putObject(params,function (err, data) {
```

```
                if(err){

                    console.log(err.toString())

                }
                  else{

                      console.log(data);

                      console.log('Successfully uploaded Image.');

                        searchFaces.searchFaceMethod(callback);

                }

            });

        });

    }
```

Camera module code

This module exposes two methods, which are used to take the reference image and the input image. Each function stores the image with separate names. Once the image is captured successfully, it's uploaded in the S3 bucket.

In Chapter 6, *Security Surveillance*, we have studied the camera module and its workings, so we will not get into the details here.

Create a file with the name CameraModuleRekognition.js and include the following code:

```
var PiCamera = require('pi-camera'),

s3Bucket = require('./S3Put');

var myCameraPhoto = new PiCamera({

  mode: 'photo',

  output: `Path of Reference Image stored on raspberry pi for IndexFaces operation `,

  width: 640,
```

```
  height: 480,

});

var myCameraPhotoTarget = new PiCamera({

  mode: 'photo',

output: ''Path of input Image stored on raspberry pi for SeacrchFacesByImage
operation `,

  width: 640,

  height: 480,

  nopreview: false,

});

var camerInUse = false;

module.exports.takePicture = function (callback){

if (camerInUse == false) {

              camerInUse = true;

 myCameraPhoto.snap()

  .then((result) => {

              console.log('Your picture was captured')

              s3Bucket.uploadToS3(callback);

              camerInUse = false;

  })

  .catch((error) => {

              console.log(error.toString());

              callback(error.toString())

  });

}
```

```
else {

        console.log('camera in use..')

        }

}

module.exports.takeTargetPicture = function (callback){

if (camerInUse == false) {

        camerInUse = true;

 myCameraPhotoTarget.snap()

  .then((result) => {

        console.log('Your picture was captured')

        s3Bucket.uploadTarget_to_S3(callback);

        camerInUse = false;

  })

  .catch((error) => {

        console.log(error.toString());

        callback(error.toString())

  });

}

else {

        console.log('camera in use..')

        }

}
```

Upload reference image module code

Now, we write the main modules for uploading the reference image, where the IR sensor detects the presence and triggers Pi to capture the image, and send it to S3, and then to Rekognition to be stored in the collection.

Create a file with the name `UploadImageIR.js` and add the following code:

```
var GPIO = require('pigpio').Gpio,

cameraModule = require('./CameraModuleRekognition'),

                    s3Bucket = require('./S3Put'),

green_LED = new GPIO(19,{mode: GPIO.OUTPUT}),

red_LED= new GPIO(17,{mode: GPIO.OUTPUT}),

IR_out= new GPIO(5,{mode: GPIO.INPUT,alert: true});

red_LED.digitalWrite(0);

green_LED.digitalWrite(0);

IR_out.on('alert', function(level, tick){

        if(level==1){

        cameraModule.takePicture(function (callback) {

                        var result = callback;

if(result == 'success'){console.log('success...!!')

                        }

        })

        console.log('IR : Imaging you..!!')

        red_LED.digitalWrite(level);

        }

        else {

                red_LED.digitalWrite(level);
```

```
                    buzzer.digitalWrite(level);

          }

    })
```

Compare image module code

Now, finally, we write the main modules to upload the face comparison, where the IR sensor detects a presence and triggers Pi to capture the image and send it to S3 and then to Rekognition, where it compares the face with the collection:

1. Create a file with the name FaceComparision.js and add the following code:

```
var GPIO = require('pigpio').Gpio,

                    cameraModule =
require('./CameraModuleRekognition'),

                    s3Bucket = require('./S3Put'),

                    green_LED = new GPIO(19,{mode:
GPIO.OUTPUT}),

                    red_LED= new GPIO(17,{mode:
GPIO.OUTPUT}),

                    IR_out= new GPIO(5,{mode:
GPIO.INPUT,alert: true});

red_LED.digitalWrite(0);

green_LED.digitalWrite(0);

          IR_out.on('alert', function(level, tick){

          if(level==1){

          cameraModule.takeTargetPicture(function (callback)
{

                              var result = callback;

                              if(result == 'success'){

console.log('Face Match Success...!!')
```

```
green_LED.digitalWrite(1);

setTimeout(function () {

green_LED.digitalWrite(0);

                                              },5000)

}

})



        console.log('IR : Imaging you..!!')

        red_LED.digitalWrite(level);

        }

        else {

                red_LED.digitalWrite(level);

        }

})
```

2. Let's now execute both modules one by one and see their output.
3. Open the Terminal and run the following command:

```
sudo npm node UploadIR.js
```

4. On successful execution, you will see output as shown in *Figure 7.30*:

```
pi@raspberrypi:~/Node_Programs $ sudo node UploadImageIR.js
IR : Imaging you..!!
Your picture was captured
{ '0': null,
  '1': { ETag: '"2ac74ee0ac15f0f0ee75375c4339fac1"' } }
{ ETag: '"2ac74ee0ac15f0f0ee75375c4339fac1"' }
Successfully uploaded Image.
{"FaceRecords":[{"Face":{"FaceId":"a1dbf250-ec2d-49ea-8c88-b66defb47cdc","Boundi
ngBox":{"Width":0.2740384638309479,"Height":0.36538460850715637,"Left":0.4290865
361690521,"Top":0.42307692766189575},"ImageId":"39028ac1-8bad-51ca-a227-a1810038
13e0","ExternalImageId":"ImagePi","Confidence":99.99894714355469},"FaceDetail":{
"BoundingBox":{"Width":0.2740384638309479,"Height":0.36538460850715637,"Left":0.
4290865361690521,"Top":0.42307692766189575},"AgeRange":{"Low":20,"High":38},"Smi
le":{"Value":false,"Confidence":94.33394622802734},"Eyeglasses":{"Value":true,"C
onfidence":99.81279754638672},"Sunglasses":{"Value":true,"Confidence":54.3241691
5893555},"Gender":{"Value":"Male","Confidence":99.92909240722656},"Beard":{"Valu
e":true,"Confidence":99.98214721679688},"Mustache":{"Value":true,"Confidence":96
.16868591308594},"EyesOpen":{"Value":false,"Confidence":85.01517486572266},"Mout
hOpen":{"Value":false,"Confidence":97.42634582519531},"Emotions":[{"Type":"CONFU
SED","Confidence":15.044111251831055},{"Type":"HAPPY","Confidence":8.68303012847
9004},{"Type":"SAD","Confidence":2.055633068084717}],"Landmarks":[{"Type":"eyeLe
ft","X":0.5013062953948975,"Y":0.5581252574920654},{"Type":"eyeRight","X":0.6068
742275238037,"Y":0.5443987250328064},{"Type":"nose","X":0.5827617049217224,"Y":0
.5604122281074524},{"Type":"mouthLeft","X":0.5378267765045166,"Y":0.683447718620
3003},{"Type":"mouthRight","X":0.6207740902900696,"Y":0.6700307726860046},{"Type
":"leftPupil","X":0.4969002604484558,"Y":0.5582542419433594},{"Type":"rightPupil
","X":0.6092422008514404,"Y":0.543851912021637},{"Type":"leftEyeBrowLeft","X":0.
4587189257144928,"Y":0.5150147080421448},{"Type":"leftEyeBrowUp","X":0.486594378
94821167,"Y":0.49258068203926086},{"Type":"leftEyeBrowRight","X":0.5194676518440
247,"Y":0.4883136749267578},{"Type":"rightEyeBrowLeft","X":0.5828322768211365,"Y
":0.4862687885761261},{"Type":"rightEyeBrowUp","X":0.6068447828292847,"Y":0.4829
351007938385},{"Type":"rightEyeBrowRight","X":0.6291886568069458,"Y":0.493092924
35646057},{"Type":"leftEyeLeft","X":0.4831494688987732,"Y":0.5672017335891724},{
"Type":"leftEyeRight","X":0.5206316113471985,"Y":0.553618311882019},{"Type":"lef
tEyeUp","X":0.4994560182094574,"Y":0.550115168094635},{"Type":"leftEyeDown","X":
0.5025722980499268,"Y":0.5638507008552551},{"Type":"rightEyeLeft","X":0.59077602
62489319,"Y":0.5438061952590942},{"Type":"rightEyeRight","X":0.6232531666755676,
"Y":0.5493690967559814},{"Type":"rightEyeUp","X":0.6069566011428833,"Y":0.537010
```

5. Previous screenshot shows the metadata (extracted features of face from image) printed on console. This metadata is stored in collection and will be used later to compare the faces.

6. Next we will run the face comparison module which will take the new input image from camera and then upload it to s3 and finally using `SearchFacesByImage` function compares the face with existing faces stored in collection:

```
sudo npm node FaceComparison.js
```

7. On successful execution, you will see output as shown in *Figure 7.31*:

This brings us to the end of this chapter.

Summary

In this chapter, we learned what is image recognition and what are the building blocks of image recognition techniques. Then, we learned about AWS image recognition and S3 services using which we developed a building access management project. In Chapter 8, *Bot Building*, we will create a Wi-Fi controlled robot car.

8
Bot Building

In this chapter, we have a task cut out to build a Wi-Fi-controlled robotic car. It will not just move forwards and backwards, but will also make left and right turns. Additionally, you will also be able to control the speed of the car using **pulse-width modulation** (**PWM**). So, let's build the bot.

We need the following hardware components to build the car:

- Car chassis (toy car)
- Two DC motors
- Four plastic tires (to be fitted with DC motor and car chassis)
- L293D motor driver IC
- LEDs (6 to 8 pcs)
- Battery bank

The following topics are covered in the chapter:

- Pulse-width modulation
- Wiring up the bot
- Executing the commands

Since we have already used DC motor, L293D IC, and LEDs in Chapter 5, *Controlling the Pi*, we will not go through them in detail again. We will concentrate on building the car structure and programming part.

Car chassis

First and foremost, the requirement for building a remote-controlled car is a power source to drive the car and Raspberry Pi, as we cannot use a wired power source, because then the wire will restrict the motion of the car. So instead, we can use a good-rating battery bank that gives 9V DC output and has long battery life.

To build a car, one of the most important requirements is its chassis and tyres. We can build the chassis ourselves using hard cardboard, or can buy one that is readily available online, or even use an existing toy car chassis if you have one.

In our case, we are using a pre-built toy car chassis fitted with four tires, and two 5V DC motors, as shown in the following photo:

Figure 8.1

The previous photo (*Figure 8.1*) shows all four tires are connected with a motor; but we need only two motors for this project.

The following diagram (*Figure 8.2*) is an animated image of our actual robotic car, with two motors connected to rear wheels, and LEDs for representing different movements:

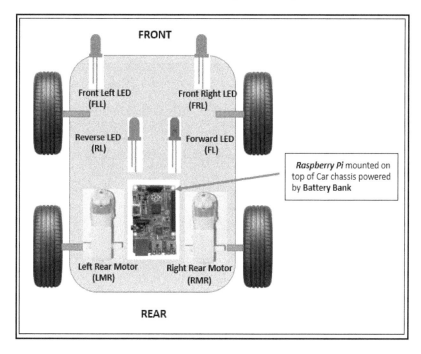

Figure 8.2

Pulse-width modulation

Before we proceed further to wire up our bot and do the programming, we will understand an important concept of PWM. In our project, PWM is used to control the speed of the DC motor.

So, what is PWM? PWM is a technique of generating an output signal from a digital source that behaves like an analog signal. It means that we can control analog circuitry or analog devices using a digital input source. This technique is used in a wide variety of applications like measurements, communication, and power control.

Let's first understand the difference between **analog** and **digital** signals.

Analog signal

An **analog signal** has continuous and varying value over any time interval, with infinite resolution in time and magnitude. A simple analog signal is a sine wave that is described using amplitude and time as shown in *Figure 8.3*:

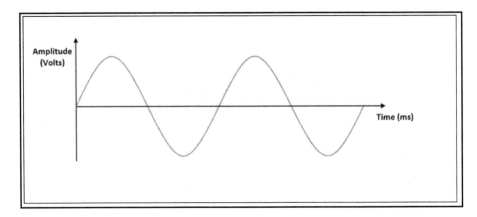

Figure 8.3

Analog signals are used for control operations of analog devices, such as controlling the speed of a DC motor (a DC motor is an analog device). To change the speed of motor we simply vary the resistance in its current path due to which current available at motor changes and hence the speed.

Let's consider that we use a battery as a source of analog signal for controlling the speed of the motor. During the operation, the output voltage and current of battery drops over a period of time, due to which the change in resistance will not change the speed of the motor in the same proportion as it was doing so earlier. Due to this varying nature of an analog signal, we will never be able to achieve the accuracy and consistency in speed control. One more disadvantage of using analog signaling in our case is that it is prone to noise, which will distort the signal and reduce the quality of transmission.

Having discussed the issues with analog signaling, it is still possible to control the operation, but it requires precision analog circuits which are bulky, costly, and consume a lot of power, which is not ideal for many use cases.

Digital signal

A **digital signal** has non-continuous and discrete value, with finite resolution in time and magnitude. Digital signal always has two states either completely on (high) or completely off (low) and magnitude of amplitude will always remain stable. A simple digital signal is represented as a square wave as shown in the following diagram:

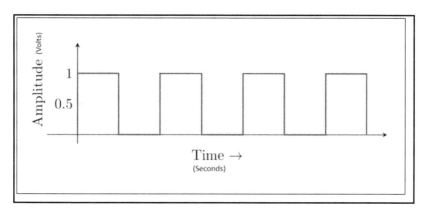

Figure 8.4

Due to the shortcomings of analog signal in control application, we use digital signal to control the same analog circuits because of the stable and discrete nature of digital signal. And here PWM comes into the picture.

PWM is a technique of generating analog signals using a digital source. PWM signals consist of mainly two components that define its behavior, one is **duty cycle** (**DC**) and another one is frequency.

Duty cycle represents the amount of time signal remains in high (on) state as a percentage of total time it takes to complete one cycle. Frequency defines how fast a signal switches between high (on) and low (off) state. For example, if the frequency of a digital signal is 100 Hz the signal will switch its state between high and low 100 times.

The following diagram shows how the digital signal behaves when the duty cycle is varied:

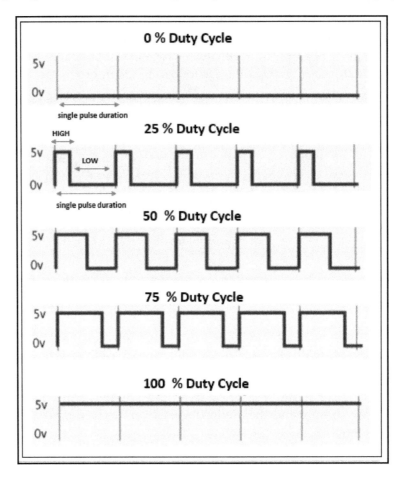

Figure 8.5

So by applying appropriate duty cycle and frequency, we can create a digital signal which will behave like a constant voltage analog signal and can be used to operate our DC motor.

The main difference between a pure analog signal and a digitally created analog signal is that pure analog signal's curve is smooth (refer *Figure 8.3*) whereas curve of a digitally created analog signal is stepping, square, and discrete in nature (refer *Figure 8.6*):

Figure 8.6

Wiring up the bot

Now let's start making the circuits required to build our Bot.

Wiring L293D with motor

First we interface both the motor of car with motor driver IC L293D as shown in the following diagram:

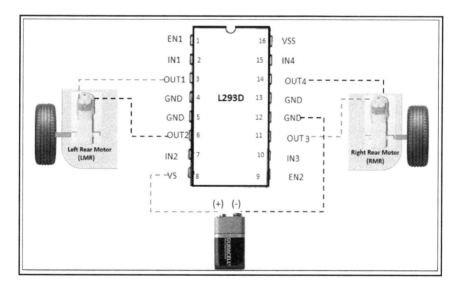

Figure 8.7

In the previous diagram:

- **OUT1** (pin 3) has been connected to one terminal of **LRM**
- **OUT2** (pin 6) has been connected to second terminal of **LRM**
- **OUT3** (pin 11) has been connected to one terminal of **RRM**
- **OUT4** (pin 14) has been connected to second terminal of **RRM**
- **VS** is connected to positive terminal of 9V DC battery
- **GND** is connected to negative terminal of 9V DC battery

The OUT pins provide DC output voltage to drive the motor. The value of voltage output of out pins is decided by the voltage applied to pin VS of L293D. In our circuit diagram we have used a 9V DC battery which will power our 9V motors (Note that this 9V battery is not used to control the speed of motor). Make sure you choose your power source precisely as per rating of motors. If a very high power source is used it can damage your motor and if underpowered, it will not drive the motor at all.

In case you don't want to use batteries, DC adaptor is a good replacement which will supply the required voltage output as per requirement.

Wiring L293D with Raspberry Pi

Now we will interface L293D with Raspberry Pi as shown in the following diagram:

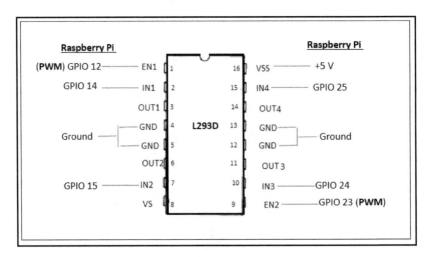

Figure 8.8

In the previous diagram:

- **GPIO 12** of Raspberry Pi is connected to enable 1 (pin 1) of L293D
- **GPIO 14** of Raspberry Pi is connected to input 1 (pin 2) of L293D
- **GPIO 15** of Raspberry Pi is connected to input 2 (pin 7) of L293D
- **GPIO 23** of Raspberry Pi is connected to enable 2 (pin 9) of L293D
- **GPIO 24** of Raspberry Pi is connected to input 3 (pin 10) of L293D
- **GPIO 25** of Raspberry Pi is connected to input 4 (pin 15) of L293D
- **VSS** of L293D is connected to 5V output from Raspberry Pi
- **GND** of L293D is connected to ground terminal of Raspberry Pi

Here enable 1 and enable 2 pin of L293D are responsible for driving the motor and using these pins we will control the speed of motor by applying PWM. PWM control the speed by providing a series of on-off pulses with varying duty cycle.

To increase the speed of motor we increase the duty cycle which in turn increases the high signal duration in single pulse compared to the duration of a low signal which results in the motor being in on state for a longer duration then off during one single pulse. Here a single pulse is a combination of on and off combined.

Let's understand our case with the following diagram:

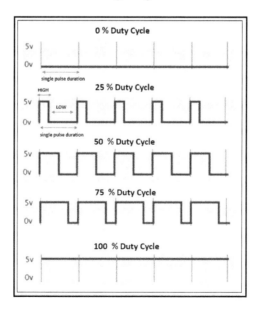

Figure 8.9

In the preceding diagram:

- **DC = 0%**: Enable voltage signal will be zero all the time
- **DC = 25%**: Enable voltage will remain high for only ¼ of the duration of a single pulse
- **DC = 50%**: Enable voltage will remain high for only ½ of duration of single pulse
- **DC = 75%**: Enable voltage will remain high for only ¾ of duration of single pulse
- **DC = 100%**: Enable voltage will remain high for full duration of single pulse

From the previous diagram, we can understand how PWM controls the speed of motor.

Now that we have completed the circuit and connections, let's write the code. Here we will implement MQTT protocol for communication between car and remote-control client.

We need Node.js runtime to be set up in Raspberry Pi and MQTT broker running on the cloud/server. Since we have already done these setups in the previous chapter so we will not repeat them here again.

Create a file with the name `car_control.js` and include `pigpio` module. This module gives access to GPIO of Raspberry Pi:

```
var GPIO = require('pigpio').Gpio;
```

Set up the GPIO in code as per connections made earlier. Here we initialize the GPIO of Raspberry Pi as per the requirement:

```
var red_LED = new GPIO(17,{mode: GPIO.OUTPUT}),
green_LED = new GPIO(5,{mode: GPIO.OUTPUT}), front_left_LED = new
GPIO(19,{mode: GPIO.OUTPUT}), front_right_LED = new GPIO(26,{mode:
GPIO.OUTPUT}), enable_1 = new GPIO(12,{mode: GPIO.OUTPUT}),
enable_2 = new GPIO(23,{mode: GPIO.OUTPUT}),
input_1 = new GPIO(14,{mode: GPIO.OUTPUT}),
input_2 = new GPIO(15,{mode: GPIO.OUTPUT}),
input_3 = new GPIO(24,{mode: GPIO.OUTPUT}),
input_4 = new GPIO(25,{mode: GPIO.OUTPUT});

var rightIndicatorHandler='', leftIndicatorHandler= '';
```

Now we will write functions for all the different movements of a car that is forward, reverse, right turn, and left turn. These functions will return a callback to the calling function as acknowledgment.

Forward movement

The right rear motor should rotate clockwise and left rear motor should rotate anticlockwise. During forward movement the green LED (marked as forward LED in *Figure 8.2*) will glow:

```
module.exports.move_forward = function(callback){
  clearInterval(leftIndicatorHandler);
  clearInterval(rightIndicatorHandler);
    enable_1.digitalWrite(1);
    input_1.digitalWrite(0);
    input_2.digitalWrite(1);

    enable_2.digitalWrite(1);
    input_3.digitalWrite(1);
    input_4.digitalWrite(0);

    green_LED.digitalWrite(1);
    red_LED.digitalWrite(0);
    console.log ("move forward")
    callback ("move forward")
}
```

Reverse movement

The right rear motor should rotate anticlockwise and left rear motor should rotate clockwise. During forward movement green LED will glow:

```
module.exports.move_reverse = function(callback){
  clearInterval(leftIndicatorHandler);
  clearInterval(rightIndicatorHandler);

  enable_1.digitalWrite(1);
  input_1.digitalWrite(1);
  input_2.digitalWrite(0);

  enable_2.digitalWrite(1);
  input_3.digitalWrite(0);
  input_4.digitalWrite(1);

  green_LED.digitalWrite(0);
  red_LED.digitalWrite(1);
  console.log ("move reverse")
  callback ("move reverse")
}
```

Right turn

The right rear motor should remain stationary and left rear motor should rotate anticlockwise:

```
module.exports.move_right = function(callback) {

    indicatorRight();
    enable_1.digitalWrite(0);
    input_1.digitalWrite(0);
    input_2.digitalWrite(0);
    enable_2.digitalWrite(1);
    input_3.digitalWrite(1);
    input_4.digitalWrite(0);
    console.log ("Turn Right")
    callback ("Turn Right")
}
```

Left turn

The right rear motor should rotate clockwise, and the left rear motor should remain stationary:

```
module.exports.move_left = function(callback){
    indicatorLeft();

    enable_1.digitalWrite(1);
    input_1.digitalWrite(0);
    input_2.digitalWrite(1);

    enable_2.digitalWrite(0);
    input_3.digitalWrite(0);
    input_4.digitalWrite(0);

    console.log ("Turn Left")
    callback ("Turn Left") }
}
```

Stop

Both the motors should remain stationary:

```
module.exports.motor_stop = function(callback){
    clearInterval(leftIndicatorHandler);
    clearInterval(rightIndicatorHandler);
```

```
enable_1.digitalWrite(0);
input_1.digitalWrite(0);
input_2.digitalWrite(0);

enable_2.digitalWrite(0);
input_3.digitalWrite(0);
input_4.digitalWrite(0);

green_LED.digitalWrite(0);
red_LED.digitalWrite(0);

console.log ("Motor Stopped")
callback ("Motor Stopped")
}
```

Speed control

This function will update the duty cycle of the enable pin of both the motors and vary the speed of rotation:

```
module.exports.motor_speed = function(pwm,callback){
  console.log(pwm)
  enable_1.pwmWrite(pwm);
  enable_2.pwmWrite(pwm);
  console.log ("speed change")
  callback("speed change")
}
```

An `indicator` function is required which will make indicator LEDs on the left front and right front of the car blink whenever car makes a turn:

```
indicatorLeft = function(){ leftIndicatorHandler = setInterval(function() {
  if(front_left_LED.digitalRead()==1){
      front_left_LED.digitalWrite(0)
    }
    else{
      front_left_LED.digitalWrite(1)
    }
  },250)
}
```

Now we will create an MQTT client for the car which will receive the commands from the MQTT broker. Here we are using EMQTT broker which is an open source and free of cost broker.

We have already done its installation and setup in an earlier chapter of this book so we will not go through it again.

Create a file with the name `car_client.js` and include the `mqtt` module and `car_control.js` module:

```
var mqtt = require('mqtt');
var motor_Dir= require ('./car_control.js ');
```

Now connect to MQTT broker running on server and subscribe to topic:

```
var options = {
                port:'1883',
                host: IP_Adress_Of_Mqtt_Broker_Server
              }

var client = mqtt.connect(options)
  client.on('connect', () => {
  client.subscribe('controlPi/cmd');
  console.log ("\r\n Raspberry Pi mqtt client connected to broker \r\n ");
})
```

Now listen on event `'message'` which is emitted when a message is received from broker. Based on the message type we execute the functions of `car_control.js` module:

```
client.on('message', (topic, message) => {
  message= message.toString();
  else if(message=='forward'){
    motor_Dir.move_forward((callback)=> {
      var Acknowledgement=callback;
      client.publish('raspbPi/ack',Acknowledgement)
    })
  }
    else if(message=='reverse'){
      motor_Dir.move_reverse((callback)=> {
        var Acknowledgement=callback;
        client.publish('raspbPi/ack',Acknowledgement)
      })
    }
    else if(message=='right'){
      motor_Dir.move_right((callback)=> {
        var Acknowledgement=callback;
        client.publish('raspbPi/ack',Acknowledgement)
```

```
    })
  }
  else if(message=='stop') {
    motor_Dir.motor_stop((callback)=> {
      var Acknowledgement=callback;
      client.publish('raspbPi/ack',Acknowledgement)
    })
  }
  else if(message=='left'){
    motor_Dir.move_left((callback)=> {
      var Acknowledgement=callback;
      client.publish('raspbPi/ack',Acknowledgement)
    })
  }
  else if(message=='64'){
    motor_Dir.motor_speed(message,(callback)=> {
      var Acknowledgement=callback;
      client.publish('raspbPi/ack',Acknowledgement)
    })
  }
  else if(message=='128'){
    motor_Dir.motor_speed(message,(callback)=> {
      var Acknowledgement=callback;
      client.publish('raspbPi/ack',Acknowledgement)
    })
  }
  else if(message=='192'){
    motor_Dir.motor_speed(message,(callback)=> {
      var Acknowledgement=callback;
      client.publish('raspbPi/ack',Acknowledgement)
    })
  }
  else if(message=='255'){
    motor_Dir.motor_speed(message,(callback)=> {
      var Acknowledgement=callback;
      client.publish('raspbPi/ack',Acknowledgement)
    })
  }
  else {
    console.log("wrong command")
  }
})
```

In the previous code we passed `64`, `128`, `192`, and `255` as the values of duty cycle to speed control method `motor_speed`. Since default value for range of duty cycle is `255`, a duty cycle of `64` is equal to 25% of full range and `128` is 50%, `192` is 75%, and `255` is 100%.

As we have completed our coding, let's execute the code. Open the terminal in Raspberry Pi and execute command `sudo node car_client.js` as shown in the following screenshot:

Figure 8.10

As our robot car is up and ready to run, let's use `MQTT.fx` client to send commands to the car remotely and see the action. `MQTT.fx` is a free and open source client tool for MQTT.

`MQTT.fx` can be downloaded from `http://emqtt.io/` as per the OS being used.

After download and installation, open the client, click on the **Settings** button and provide connection details and then connect. Once connected we will subscribe to topic `raspbPi/ack` on which we will get acknowledgment from the car.

Now we will **Publish** commands to make our car move.

Before we start to publish our commands to car we must subscribe to topic
`raspbPi/ack` on which the acknowledgement from car (Raspberry Pi) will be received as
shown in the following screenshot:

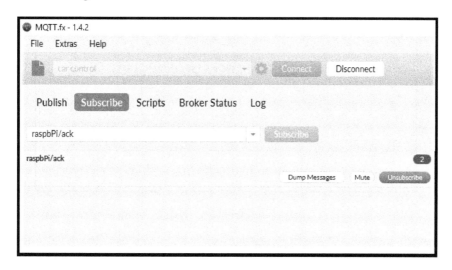

Figure 8.11

Executing the commands

Let's now start sending the commands from `MQTT.fx` client and see our car in motion.

To move forward, we publish the message `forward` on topic `controlPi/cmd` as shown
in *Figure 8.12*.

Command:

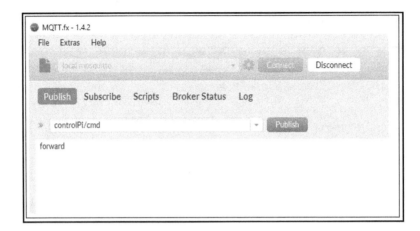

Figure 8.12

On the **Subscribe** tab we will see the message `move forward` as acknowledgment sent back from the car as a confirmation that the car is moving forward now. Refer to the following screenshot:

Acknowledgment:

Figure 8.13

To move backward/reverse we publish command `reverse`; the car will start moving in a backward direction, the red LED will glow and on the **Subscribe** tab we will see the message move reverse.

Command:

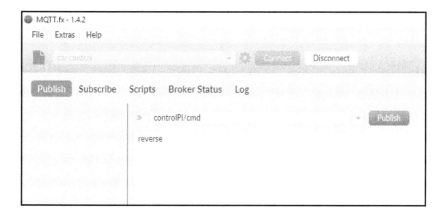

Figure 8.14

Acknowledgment:

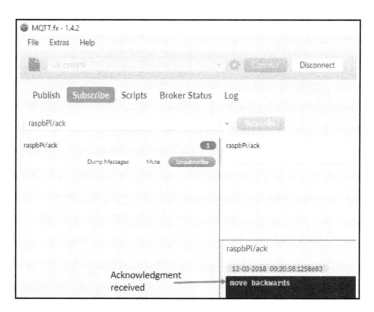

Figure 8.15

To make a right turn **Publish** message `right`; the car will make a right turn and the right side indicator will blink. On the **Subscribe** tab we will receive the message `Turn Right`.

Command:

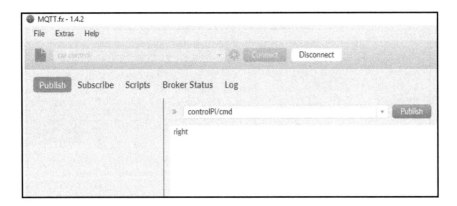

Figure 8.16

Acknowledgment:

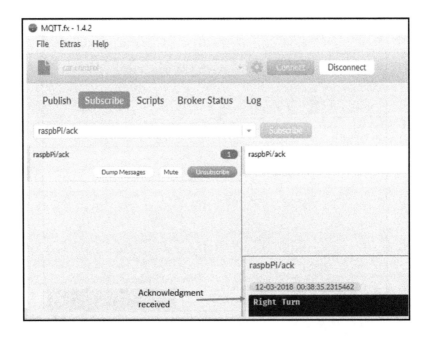

Figure 8.17

To make a left turn **Publish** the message `left`; the car will make a the left turn and left side indicator will blink. On the **Subscribe** tab we will receive the message `Turn Left`.

Command:

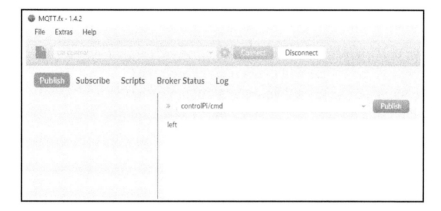

Figure 8.18

Acknowledgment:

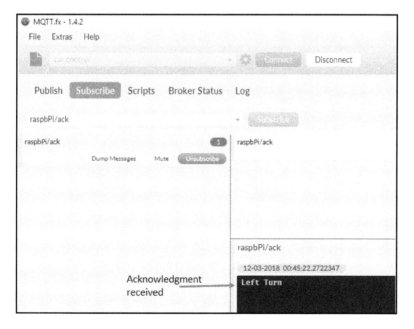

Figure 8.19

The resolution of the PWM signal is 255 by default which indicates that to run the motor at maximum speed, duty cycle of the PWM signal will need to be set at 255 that is the signal will remain high throughout.

To change the speed of the car we will modify the value of the duty cycle. Please note that value of duty cycle should not go beyond the maximum resolution of the PWM signal which is 255 in our case:

- If we publish message as 64, car will move at 1/4 of top speed
- If message is 128, car will move at 1/2 of top speed
- If message is 192, car will move at 3/4 of top speed
- And when message is 255, car will move at top speed

Command:

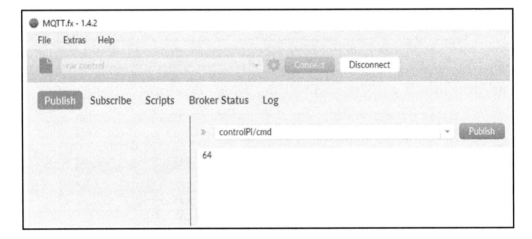

Figure 8.20

Acknowledgment:

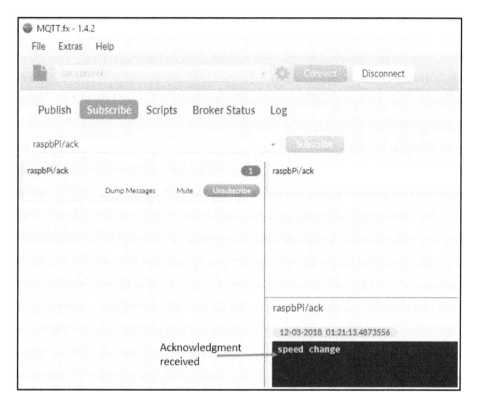

Figure 8.21

Summary

Finally, we come to the end of this chapter and we have built our own IoT-enabled robotic car which can be controlled remotely. The car has all the basic moves like forward motion, backward motion, and it is also capable of taking turns. We also learnt about PWM and how it helps to control the speed of an analog DC motor using digital signal.

In Chapter 9, *Security in IoT*, we will study the most important aspect of IoT security of an IoT ecosystem. Without a secure and protected ecosystem our services and products will be vulnerable to hacking and cyber-attacks which can cause huge losses to people and business. So let's get ready to secure your IoT ecosystem in Chapter 9, *Security in IoT*.

9
Security in IoT

At the beginning of this book, we learned how IoT has captured headlines across the world. Every news article and piece of research about it describes how it can transform our daily lives. An IoT ecosystem with its smart sensor-enabled devices that communicate with each other over the internet provides immense opportunities for conducting business, providing healthcare, managing city resources, and facilitating the management of transportation and other infrastructures.

The rapid growth of the IoT ecosystem is now being challenged by security experts, and rightly so. Imagine billions of devices connected to the internet and running without appropriate security measures. It is like an open invitation to hackers who can take control of less-secure devices, and then we will be at their mercy. These devices may include highly critical medical equipment, lockers with valuable items, connected vehicles, city infrastructure, and others, which at any cost cannot be left out in the open for hackers to get access to. For example, medical equipment such as drug diffusion pumps are at risk, which could be hacked to alter the diffusion rate of drugs inside the body, which is a life-threatening situation for a patient. In case of internet-connected vehicles, a hacker can take control of the vehicle and drive to any location or may cause an accident. We also have one famous case of connected vehicles being hacked, where two experts demonstrated the security loopholes in a jeep and took complete control over the car remotely. You can check out the video of this hack on YouTube by visiting `https://www.youtube.com/watch?v=MK0SrxBC1xs`.

So, the security in IoT becomes the central and most important pillar of an IoT ecosystem and if we do not discuss IoT security here, then this book will remain incomplete. Let's now discuss the following topics in this chapter:

- Loopholes in IoT ecosystem
- The challenges in providing security in IoT
- Generic solutions to IoT security issues
- Security solutions for Raspberry Pi

The challenges in providing IoT security

More and more IoT devices are being deployed every day, making IoT systems more complex than ever. This leads to increased difficulty level in securing IoT systems. In the upcoming subsections, we will speak about the most common problems that are being faced today.

Security in endpoint devices – constrained devices

Most of our endpoint devices (constrained) that constitute the sensors, actuators, and controllers don't have enough memory or processing power, and run on low and limited power. Due to these reasons, traditional security approaches cannot be applied to these constrained devices because they use heavy encryption and decryption algorithms that require high processing power, a lot of memory, and power to facilitate the computations in real time.

The solution for this is we can make use of embedded encryption and decryption techniques that are an integral part of sensors and controllers itself. Also, we can put the devices on separate networks and use firewalls to overcome their limitations.

Authorization and authentication

With the large number of devices connected to the internet, it is important that only authentic devices should have authorization to participate in the network. Often, these basic requirements are largely unmet or have weak password policies that make these devices prone to attacks.

The solution is to make sure that a device that participates in the network is authentic and has correct authorization is that we should make use of SSL certificates at both the device and application level, dual authentication, such as password and SMS (or in-app passcodes), biometric signatures, and such others.

Device firmware upgrade

Updating the firmware and software of IoT devices and gateways for adding or upgrading security features is quite challenging in itself. This process is sometimes called **Firmware Over The Air** (**FOTA**).

Since the number of devices can be huge, it becomes difficult to keep track of current software/firmware versions of all the devices and what updates are available for all of them. There can be different types of devices present in the same network that runs completely different software and firmware, which can increase the complexity of the upgrade process.

In some cases, the devices are in a completely different network that supports different protocols, which is an added challenge to the existing ones.

Many of the devices may not have a FOTA facility, so the device needs to be upgraded by a technician at the device location itself or by getting the device to the service station. This causes the device to be absent from the network completely, which might impact the business and is not favorable.

In the case of consumer devices, the right to update the device software is left with the owner and if the owner opts out of upgrading, the device might be left prone to attacks.

Another case is when the device is manufactured by some third-party vendor and they stop producing that particular model, even in this case it throws a challenge to upgrade.

The solution for most of these issues is to have a device manager application that keeps a record of all the devices, along with their software and firmware versions. For devices that have a FOTA facility, the device manager application automatically upgrades the device whenever there is a newer version available and in case the upgrade fails, it rolls back to a previous stable version of the software.

For the devices that don't have FOTA, keep the software simple and minimal, to perform the basic actions required, and the rest of the complex computation can be done using gateway devices to which it connects, and a gateway device enables connectivity to the internet. The gateway devices are more sophisticated and have FOTA as well.

Secure communication

Communication that takes place between device and applications or cloud services should be secured. Most times, such communication is not at all encrypted, which makes it easy for hackers to get access to actual data that might be of importance such as medical data, bank-related data, or even something related to a nation's security. So, network security is of utmost importance.

The solution is to make use of **Transport Level Security (TLS) / Secured Sockets Layer (SSL)** certificates at the device and application/cloud level to encrypt the data before sending it. We can set up private networks as well for isolating devices from public. These cloud service providers give additional security features as part of their services, which can be used to further enhance the security of the IoT system.

Data security

When a large number of devices are connected to the internet, they generate huge volumes of valuable data. Data such as medical information, bank-related information, or maybe information that is important to an organization and nation can be of personal interest to someone. Most times, this data is stored in less secured storage systems and human-readable formats, without any encryption or digital signatures. This makes the data easily available to unwanted people and poses a huge risk to a person and organization.

The solution is that all user and sensor data generated by the IoT system should be stored in a highly secured data storage system, which should be guarded by firewalls, should be inside private networks, and should not be available to the outside world over the internet. The data should not be stored with the identity of its owner wherever possible. The owner of the data should have the option to share their data with the service provider for further services.

High availability

Keeping the IoT system up and running with almost zero downtime is extremely important. Critical applications such as medical equipment, traffic control signals, and power grids are implementing IoT. The high availability of IoT applications that include end devices, gateway devices, mobile and desktop applications and cloud services becomes of paramount importance.

The solution is to make sure we have our systems up and running all the time. The implementation of an IoT system should take advantage of multicluster architecture, where we have one primary and multiple secondary systems running, which are in sync. In case of the failure of the primary systems, the secondary system takes the lead and becomes the primary without any downtime and keeps the system running.

Identifying cyber attacks

Cyber attacks are sometimes disguised as one of the legitimate nodes in a network, which retrieves important information and then suddenly starts attacking the system. Due to the large number of devices, multiple networks, different protocols, and varied working nature of multiple sensors, it becomes difficult to identify when the attack takes place.

We can deploy solutions to monitor all the networks to detect anomalies, check the logs of the communication that takes place between devices and applications, perform penetration testing, identify which devices are compromised, and see what data has been stolen, all in a timely manner. Once we identify the issues, we must apply security patches and updates to avoid them in the future and implement advanced machine learning and analytics techniques that can predict and be used as an alert in advance in case of possible threats.

Absence of standards

IoT has picked up in the last few years, but we lack the standards for its implementation. Each and every implementation is different from another in some aspects. An IoT system is made up of multiple components combined together, which include the hardware, networks, mobile platforms, and cloud services. Each component itself has multiple layers and multiple ways of implementation. For example, a mobile application can be a native mobile app or a hybrid one—both have their own technology stack. Similarly, a gateway device can be a Raspberry Pi or a custom one, and a server can be in the cloud or on premises.

Having so many differences, it becomes next to impossible to have a set standard of security in IoT because one set of security features may work in one case and fail in another.

As of today, it is difficult to have one solution for all the problems but organizations across the world are getting together to form IoT alliances for setting up IoT standards. Since these will take some time to come into effect, we should try to establish best practices for implementing each component of the IoT system until then.

Ignorance from customers and manufactures

Most IoT products are sold by highlighting a long list of some cool and exciting features, in which security comes last and sometimes is not on the list at all. Many researchers have shown that security is considered just another feature of the product for which consumers are not willing to pay a premium, which in turn doesn't encourage the product manufacturers to put extra effort and cost into adding the necessary security features. This ignorance toward security can prove to be a disaster for both the consumer and product manufacturers in the long run.

The least that can be done by the product manufactures is to make security the heart of every solution. Whenever a new product is designed, security features should be given topmost priority and the rest of the features should be designed around it, instead of having security as an optional add-on feature. Also, an extra effort is required to make customers aware of the importance of security. This should become a standard practice across the industry so that customers never opt out of the security features, whether deliberately or in ignorance.

Trends and challenges in specific industries

Every industry that is adapting IoT has its own security challenges, which vary a lot from other industries and obviously require a different set of solutions. Let's examine the cases for a few popular industries, such as smart homes and buildings, industrial, and automotive.

Automotive industries

As per recent studies done in the automotive industry, there are more than 200 million cars that have internet connectivity in some form or other and in the next few years, automobiles will be the largest industry in adopting IoT. Among connected products, the number of cars will be highest.

This development will have a dual impact on the automotive industry, one from the consumer's perspective and the other one from OEMs (the car manufacturers). The consumer will have the benefits of continuous internet-connected car infotainment, navigation, location tracking, and other remote control features.

OEMs will be the major beneficiary of the impact of IoT on the automotive industry. The manufacturer will be able to have enough information about its customers to provide customized services such as predictive maintenance, where they can alert the customer in advance of any component failure and provide repairs and replacements, remotely run diagnostics for any issues, and provide over-the-air software updates without having to recall all defective cars. All the data collected from connected cars helps the OEM to improve the cars over a period of time.

There are numerous benefits of IoT, but there are many challenges as well. Increased connectivity of cars will generate a huge amount of data for OEMs. There is increased responsibility placed on OEMs to protect this data securely. The users will connect their cars with their smart phones, which will sync their phone and its data to the car, which will potentially be available for hackers and poses a serious threat. These issues can be kept in check by making sure that all data is kept with the OEM itself and not with another vendor or IoT service provider. Follow best practices for security and do the necessary encryption and isolation of data from the rest of the IT system.

Apart from security issues, another major issue that automobile manufacturers are facing is domain expertise. Traditionally, these manufactures don't have strong internal IT departments as it had little role to play. But with advancement in automobiles such as connected cars, autonomous cars, electric cars, IT has become a major component. To overhaul the entire organization for the next wave of automobiles, manufacturers need to put in a lot of effort, time, and money.

Smart homes and buildings

Only a few years ago, our homes, offices, and commercial buildings offered basic facilities such as heating, ventilation, cooling, lighting, access control, and firefighting systems with basic provision of controls. These systems usually had a central control room, which needs continuous monitoring by service engineers throughout the day to look after all the issues passively.

With the increased threat of global warming and depleting natural resources, there is high demand for reducing the power consumption of buildings, making them self-sustainable, safe, and smart with minimum human intervention. Now, we have solar-powered buildings fitted with smart meters that monitor and optimize power consumption, hence reducing their carbon footprint and electricity bills.

Smart buildings and homes are not just limited to saving energy, but have all sorts of sophisticated automation systems that help in performing daily operations with minimal interference. Operations such as security checking and access management are taken care of by machine learning techniques, where people recognized by the system get access to their home or work. Heating, ventilation, and cooling systems are adjusted automatically using multiple sensors and external climatic conditions.

Advancement in home and building infrastructure comes with a lot of risk. We have seen in the recent past that many smart and connected homes and buildings came under cyberattack which led to chaotic situations. Slight lapses in security can result in dangerous outcomes especially in cases where the targets are hospitals, defense facilities, and government offices.

Traditionally, the building and home management systems were part of the **Industrial Control System** (**ICS**), but today's smart building and home management systems are completely different and should not be treated as the same line when we talk about security and their operation. Smart buildings are much more open and connected in comparison to ICS and IoT sensors, and gateway devices are considered as part of automation system instead of an ICS. So, it is required to have a dedicated security plan for IoT-based systems that follows industry standards and best practices.

Securing Raspberry Pi

We have done a lot of discussing regarding security in IoT in general, and discussed few specific use cases such as automobiles, smart buildings, and home automation. However, now we will focus on securing our Raspberry Pi, which we have been using throughout the book to build different projects.

There are many ways to secure our Raspberry Pi, so we will learn how to implement and enable these security features and make our Pi secure.

Changing the default password

Every Raspberry Pi that is running the Raspbian operating system has the default username `pi` and default password `raspberry`, which should be changed as soon as we boot up the Pi for the first time. If our Raspberry Pi is exposed to the internet and the default username and password has not been changed, then it becomes an easy target for hackers.

To change the password of the Pi in case you are using the GUI for logging in, open the menu and go to **Preferences** and **Raspberry Pi Configuration**, as shown in *Figure 10.1*:

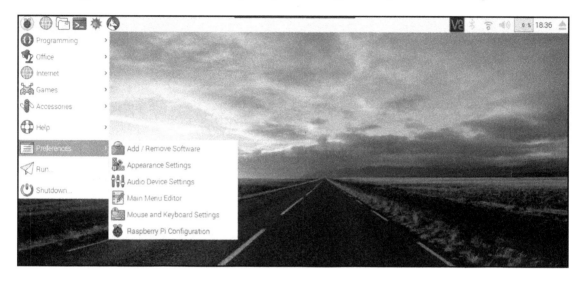

Figure 10.1

Within Raspberry Pi Configuration under the **System** tab, select the change password option, which will prompt you to provide a new password. After that, click on **OK** and the password is changed (refer *Figure 10.2*):

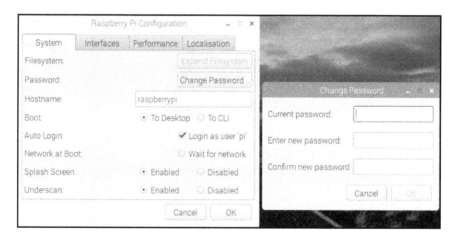

Figure 10.2

If you are logging in through PuTTY using SSH, then open the configuration setting by running the `sudo raspi-config` command, as shown in *Figure 10.3*:

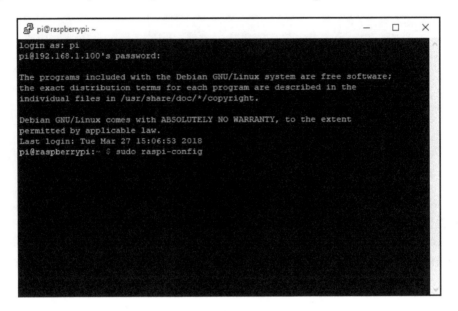

Figure 10.3

On successful execution of the command, the configuration window opens up. Then, select the second option to change the password and finish, as shown in *Figure 10.4*:

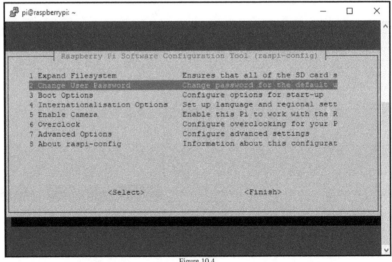

Figure 10.4

It will prompt you to provide a new password; you just need to provide it and exit. Then, the new password is set. Refer to *Figure 10.5*:

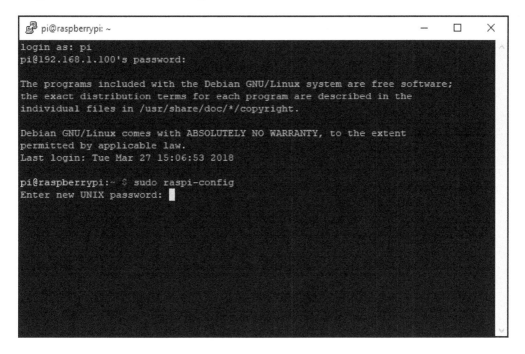

Figure 10.5

Changing the username

All Raspberry Pis come with the default username pi, which should be changed to make it more secure. We create a new user and assign it all rights, and then delete the pi user.

To add a new user, run the `sudo adduser adminuser` command in the terminal. It will prompt for a password; provide it, and you are done, as shown in *Figure 10.6*:

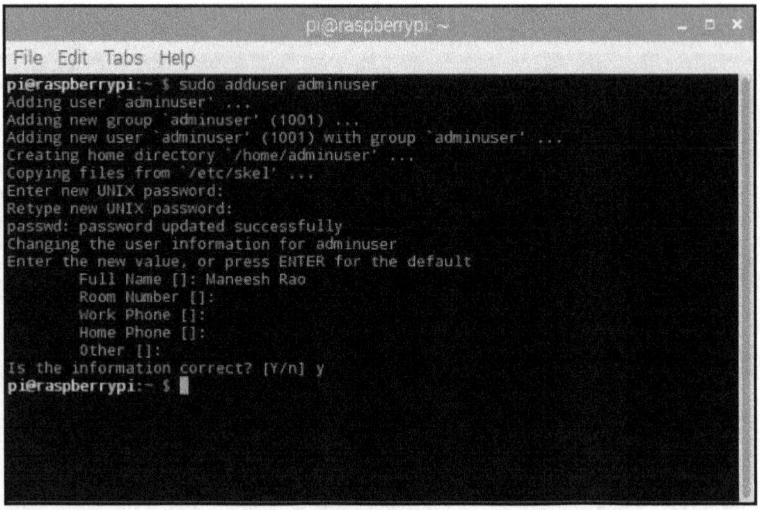

Figure 10.6

Now, we will add our newly created user to the `sudo` group so that it has all the root-level permissions, as shown in *Figure 10.7*:

Figure 10.7

Now, we can delete the default user, `pi`, by running the `sudo deluser pi` command. This will delete the user, but its repository folder `/home/pi` will still be there. If required, you can delete that as well.

Making sudo require a password

When a command is run with `sudo` as the prefix, then it'll execute it with superuser privileges. By default, running a command with `sudo` doesn't need a password, but this can cost dearly if a hacker gets access to Raspberry Pi and takes control of everything. To make sure that a password is required every time a command is run with superuser privileges, edit the `010_pi-nopasswd` file under `/etc/sudoers.d/` by executing the command shown in *Figure 10.8*:

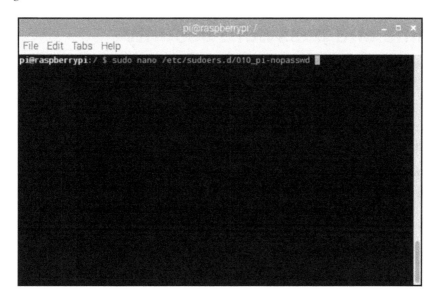

Figure 10.8

This command will open up the file in the `nano` editor; replace the content with `pi ALL=(ALL) PASSWD: ALL`, and save it.

Updated Raspbain operating system
To get the latest security updates, it is important to ensure that the
Raspbian OS is updated with the latest version whenever available. Visit
`https://www.raspberrypi.org/documentation/raspbian/updating.md` to
learn the steps to update Raspbain.

Improving SSH security

SSH is one of the most common techniques to access Raspberry Pi over the network and it
becomes necessary to use if you want to make it secure.

Username and password security

Apart from having a strong password, we can allow and deny access to specific users. This
can be done by making changes in the `sshd_config` file. Run the `sudo nano`
`/etc/ssh/sshd_config` command.

This will open up the `sshd_config` file; then, add the following line(s) at the end to allow
or deny specific users:

- **To allow users, add the line**: `AllowUsers tom john merry`
- **To deny users, add this line**: `DenyUsers peter methew`

For these changes to take effect, it is necessary to reboot the Raspberry Pi.

Key-based authentication

Using a public-private key pair for authenticating a client to an SSH server (Raspberry Pi),
we can secure our Raspberry Pi from hackers. To enable key-based authentication, we first
need to generate a public-private key pair using tools called PuTTYgen for Windows and
ssh-keygen for Linux. Note that a key pair should be generated by the client and not by
Raspberry Pi. For our purpose, we will use PuTTYgen for generating the key pair.
Download PuTTY from the following web link:

`https://www.putty.org/`

Note that puTTYgen comes with PuTTY, so you need not install it separately.

Open the puTTYgen client and click on **Generate**, as shown in *Figure 10.9*:

Figure 10.9

Next, we need to hover the mouse over the blank area to generate the key, as highlighted in *Figure 10.10*:

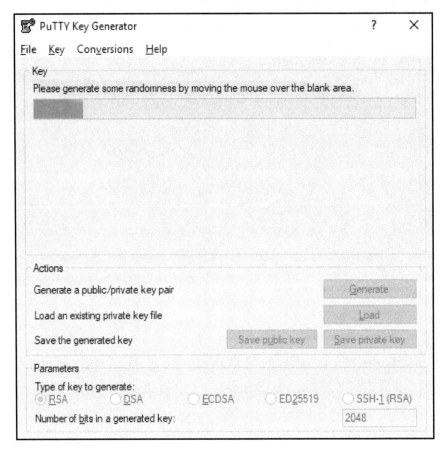

Figure 10.10

Once the key generation process is complete, there will be an option to save the public and private keys separately for later use, as shown in *Figure 10.11*—ensure you keep your private key safe and secure:

Figure 10.11

Let's name the public key file `rpi_pubkey`, and the private key file `rpi_privkey.ppk` and transfer the public key file `rpi_pubkey` from our system to Raspberry.

Log in to Raspberry Pi and under the user repository, which is /home/pi in our case, create a special directory with the name .ssh, as shown in *Figure 10.12*:

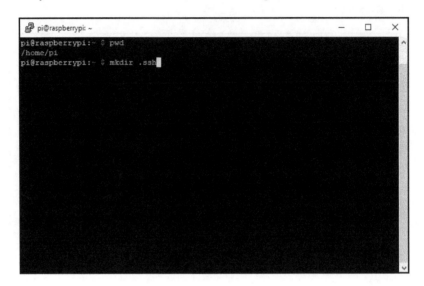

Figure 10.12

Now, move into the .ssh directory using the cd command and create/open the file with the name authorized_keys, as shown in *Figure 10.13*:

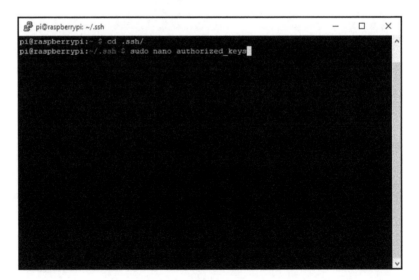

Figure 10.13

The `nano` command opens up the `authorized_keys` file in which we will copy the content of our public key file, `rpi_pubkey`. Then, save (*Ctrl + O*) and close the file (*Ctrl + X*).

Now, provide the required permissions for your `pi` user to access the files and folders. Run the following commands to set permissions:

```
chmod 700 ~/.ssh/ (set permission for .ssh directory)
chmod 600 ~/.ssh/authorized_keys (set permission for key file)
```

Refer to *Figure 10.14*, which shows the permissions before and after running the `chmod` commands:

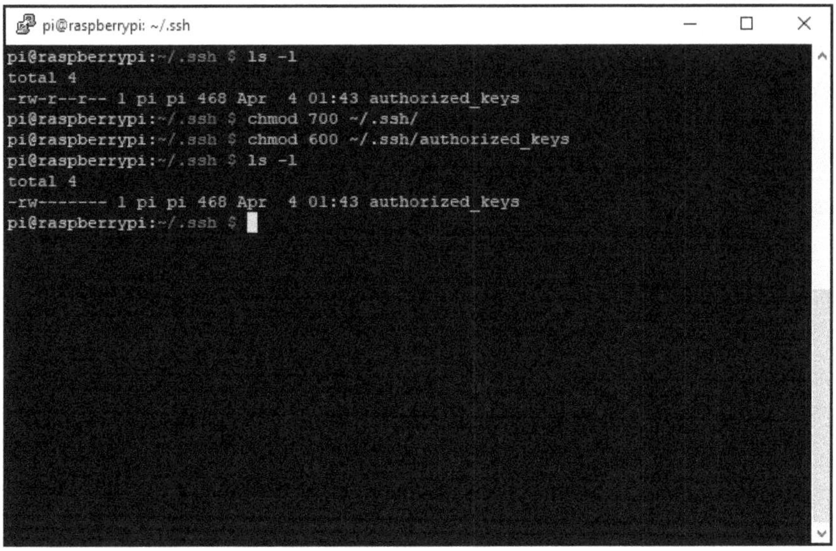

Figure 10.14

Finally, we need to disable the password logins to avoid unauthorized access by editing the `/etc/ssh/sshd_config` file. Open the file in the `nano` editor by running the following command:

```
sudo nano etc/ssh/sshd_config
```

In the file, there is a parameter `#PasswordAuthentication yes`. We need to uncomment the line by removing `#` and setting the value to `no`:

```
PasswordAuthentication no
```

Save (*Ctrl* + *O*) and close the file (*Ctrl* + X). Now, password login is prohibited and we can access the Raspberry Pi using the key file only.

Restart Raspberry Pi to make sure all the changes come into effect with the following command:

```
sudo reboot
```

Here, we are assuming that both Raspberry Pi and the system that is being used to log in to Pi are one and the same.

Now, you can log in to Raspberry Pi using PuTTY. Open the PuTTY terminal and provide the IP address of your Pi. On the left-hand side of the PuTTY window, under **Category**, expand **SSH** as shown in *Figure 10.15*:

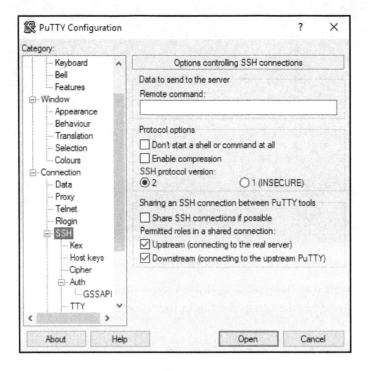

Figure 10.15

Then, select **Auth**, which will provide the option to browse and upload the private key file, as shown in *Figure 10.16*:

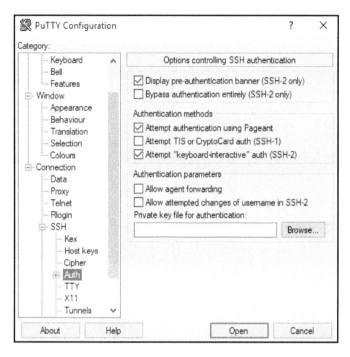

Figure 10.16

Once the private key file is uploaded, click on **Open** and it will log in to Raspberry Pi successfully without any password.

Setting up a firewall

There are many firewall solutions available for Linux/Unix-based operating systems, such as Raspbian OS in the case of Raspberry Pi. These firewall solutions have IP tables underneath to filter packets coming from different sources and allow only the legitimate ones to enter the system. IP tables are installed in Raspberry Pi by default, but are not set up. It is a bit tedious to set up the default IP table. So, we will use an alternate tool, **Uncomplicated Fire Wall** (**UFW**), which is extremely easy to set up and use `ufw`.

To install `ufw`, run the following command (refer to *Figure 10.17*):

```
sudo apt install ufw
```

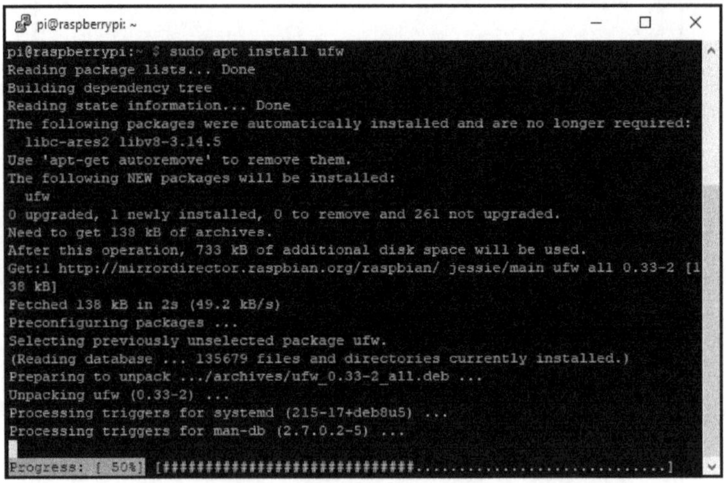

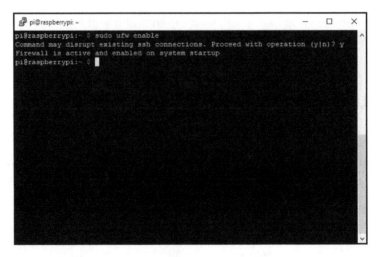

Figure 10.17

Once the download is complete, enable `ufw` (refer to *Figure 10.18*) with the following command:

```
sudo ufw enable
```

Figure 10.18

If you want to disable the firewall (refer to *Figure 10.20*), use the following command:

```
sudo ufw disable
```

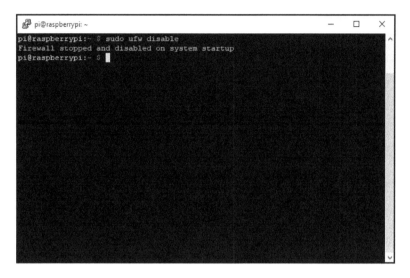

Figure 10.19

Now, let's see some features of `ufw` that we can use to improve the safety of Raspberry Pi.

Allow traffic only on a particular port using the `allow` command, as shown in *Figure 10.21*:

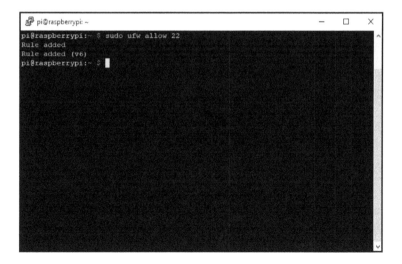

Figure 10.20

Restrict access on a port using the deny command, as shown in *Figure 10.22*:

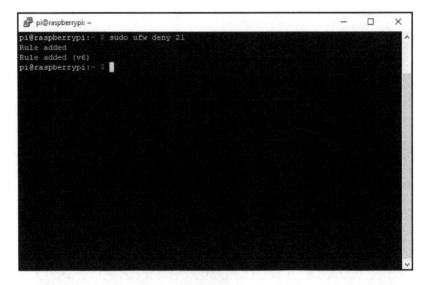

Figure 10.21

We can also allow and restrict access for a specific service on a specific port. Here, we will allow tcp traffic on port 21 (refer to *Figure 10.23*):

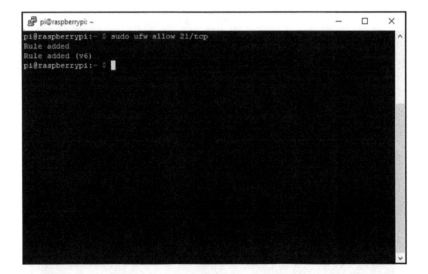

Figure 10.22

We can check the status of all the rules under the firewall using the `status` command, as shown in *Figure 10.24*:

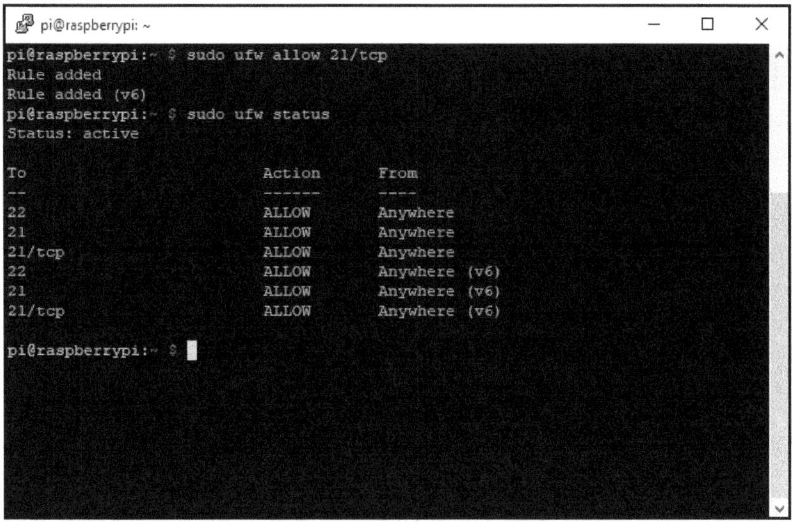

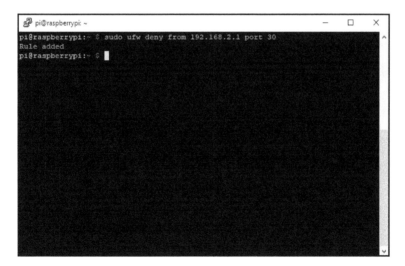

Figure 10.23

Restrict access for particular IP addresses from a particular port. Here, we deny access to `port 30` from the IP address `192.168.2.1`, as shown in *Figure 10.25*:

Figure 10.24

To learn more about ufw, visit `https://www.linux.com/learn/introduction-uncomplicated-firewall-ufw`.

Fail2Ban

At times, we use our Raspberry Pi as a server, which interacts with other devices that act as a client for Raspberry Pi. In such scenarios, we need to open certain ports and allow certain IP addresses to access them. These access points can become entry points for hackers to get hold of Raspberry Pi and do damage.

To protect ourselves from this threat, we can use the `fail2ban` tool. This tool monitors the logs of Raspberry Pi traffic, keeps a check on brute-force attempts and DDOS attacks, and informs the installed firewall to block a request from that particular IP address.

To install Fail2Ban, run the following command:

```
sudo apt install fail2ban
```

Once the download is completed successfully, a folder with the name `fail2ban` is created at path `/etc`. Under this folder, there is a file named `jail.conf`. Copy the content of this file to a new file and name it `jail.local`. This will enable `fail2ban` on Raspberry Pi. To copy, you can use the following command:

```
sudo /etc/fail2ban/jail.conf /etc/fail2ban/jail.local
```

Now, edit the file using the `nano` editor:

```
sudo nano /etc/fail2ban/jail.local
```

Look for the [ssh] section. It has a default configuration, as shown in *Figure 10.26*:

```
[ssh]
enabled  = true
port     = ssh
filter   = sshd
logpath  = /var/log/auth.log
maxretry = 6
```

Figure 10.25

This shows that Fail2Ban is enabled for ssh. It checks the port for ssh connections, filters the traffic as per conditions set under in the `sshd` configuration file located at path `etcfail2banfilters.dsshd.conf`, parses the logs at `/var/log/auth.log` for any suspicious activity, and allows only six retries for login, after which it restricts that particular IP address.

The default action taken by `fail2ban` in case someone tries to hack is defined in `jail.local`, as shown in *Figure 10.27*:

```
# Default banning action (e.g. iptables, iptables-new,
# iptables-multiport, shorewall, etc) It is used to def
# action_* variables. Can be overridden globally or per
# section within jail.local file
banaction = iptables-multiport
```

Figure 10.26

This means when the `iptables-multiport` action is taken against any malicious activity, it runs as per the configuration in `/etc/fail2ban/action.d/iptables-multiport.conf`.

Summary

In this chapter, we covered some of the steps that we can take to secure Raspberry Pi and the applications that are dependent on it. We also discussed how IoT is taking over every major industry and market in the world and why security is the most important pillar of an IoT ecosystem. Then, we discussed security challenges and their solutions in general and saw a few industry-specific examples. Finally, we discussed how the security of Raspberry Pi can be improved.

Other Books You May Enjoy

If you enjoyed this book, you may be interested in these other books by Packt:

Raspberry Pi 3 Projects for Java Programmers

Pradeeka Seneviratne, John Sirach

ISBN: 978-1-78646-212-1

- Use presence detection using the integrated bluetooth chip
- Automatic light switch using presence detection
- Use a centralized IoT service to publish data using RPC
- Control a robot by driving motors using PWM
- Create a small web service capable of performing actions on the Raspberry Pi and supply readings
- Image capture using Java together with the OpenCV framework

Raspberry Pi 3 Home Automation Projects

Shantanu Bhadoria, Ruben Oliva Ramos

ISBN: 978-1-78328-387-3

- Integrate different embedded microcontrollers and development boards like Arduino, ESP8266, Particle Photon and Raspberry Pi 3, creating real life solutions for day to day tasks and home automation
- Create your own magic mirror that lights up with useful information as you walk up to it
- Create a system that intelligently decides when to water your garden and then goes ahead and waters it for you
- Use the Wi-fi enabled Adafruit ESP8266 Huzzah to create your own networked festive display lights
- Create a simple machine learning application and build a parking automation system using Raspberry Pi
- Learn how to work with AWS cloud services and connect your home automation to the cloud
- Learn how to work with Windows IoT in Raspberry Pi 3 and build your own Windows IoT Face Recognition door locking system

Leave a review - let other readers know what you think

Please share your thoughts on this book with others by leaving a review on the site that you bought it from. If you purchased the book from Amazon, please leave us an honest review on this book's Amazon page. This is vital so that other potential readers can see and use your unbiased opinion to make purchasing decisions, we can understand what our customers think about our products, and our authors can see your feedback on the title that they have worked with Packt to create. It will only take a few minutes of your time, but is valuable to other potential customers, our authors, and Packt. Thank you!

Index

CPSIA information can be obtained
at www.ICGtesting.com
Printed in the USA
BVHW01s1625070518
515500BV00019B/1022/P